ACTIVATE
LION
MODE

BY
~~JUDY HOWARD~~
Sportster The Cat

JUDY HOWARD

**Library of Congress Control Number: 2016907363
CreateSpace Independent Publishing Platform, North Charleston, SC**

ACTIVATE LION MODE

Other Books by Judy Howard

The Cat and the Ghost Series
COAST TO COAST WITH A CAT AND A GHOST
GOING HOME WITH A CAT AND A GHOST

The Masada Series
MASADA'S MARINE
MASADA'S MISSION

Books GHOST WRITTEN BY
Sportster The Cat

The Feline Fury Series
ACTIVATE LION MODE

JUDY HOWARD

ACTIVATE LION MODE is a work of fiction. All incidents and dialogue, and all characters are products of the author's imagination and are not to be construed as real. When real life historical, or public figures, or places appear, the situations, incidents and dialogue are not intended to depict actual events or to change the entire fictional nature of this work. In all other respects, any resemblance to persons or places is entirely coincidental.

ACTIVATE LION MODE

ACKNOWLEDGMENTS

Offering my acknowledgement to you, Jessica, seems such a shallow act. I loved you. It is my plea to the universe that your tragic contribution to this story will be heard

I would be remiss if I failed to mention author David S. McCabe, who's novel, *Without Sin,* moved me beyond my safe, innocent reality and spurred me to also bring attention to the newest threat to our society, human trafficking.

Rachel Lloyd, author of , *"Girls Like Us,"* thank you for your powerful words which helped me translate this all too common story into one of .understanding and compassion.

And of course to you, Sportster The Cat, who related your story, with charm and distinguished comedy, if there is such a thing.
As always, thank you all who contributed to make this book come alive to the reader.
It takes a village of readers to make a writer.

JUDY HOWARD

DEDICATION

"They don't understand "girls like me. There are no good stories to tell."
Jessica

This book is dedicated to Jessica and to all the girls like her, who have followed in her high heels.

ACTIVATE LION MODE

BY

~~JUDY HOWARD~~

Sportster The Cat

CHAPTER ONE

My eyes sprang open. The hair on my back stood on end. Judy's scream pierced my ears, and joined the howls of the protesting motor home. My sleek graceful body slammed against the windshield. Outside, the screech of the tires orchestrated with the strange sounds of groaning metal and crackling fiberglass. Our sanctuary lurched off the road, airborne, like the birds I envied. The windshield, which insulated me from the dangers of the outside world crammed painfully against my ribs. Jagged lines crawled and crunched across my once, unobstructed view, while branches, rocks, and dirt spewed up and pounded the varicose pattern. The glass wall of security gave way.

Judy and I sailed as if we would meet the heavens. In flight, I puffed myself up to twice my size. The shattered windshield no longer protected me, and the wind penetrated through every raised hair follicle. The motorhome's flight ended with a crashing jolt. Its wheels squashed onto the ground, and the tires exploded. My paws grabbed at the air as I flew from my perch on the dashboard. I sailed past broken glass, away from our home, and through the forest's first line of pines. My body continued its line of flight soaring through green scented air, not like the birds I had coveted, but rather like a hawk on its deadly dive to earth for prey. I landed with a force, which pushed out a trumpeted lion's roar from my lungs – a last-stand challenge. Fury chased the boiling fear swelling within my chest. My bellow, to defy the wild, went unheard, smothered by the only sound the rain forest allowed – silence.

My name is Sportster. Moments before the accident I had lain, stretched out on my usual spot across the motorhome's dash, lulled by the engine's purr. Life was good. Judy, my companion, who attended to my every need, chauffeured our home on wheels.

She reached up, patted my head, as she expertly steered the motorhome onto the highway. "It's time to say goodbye to the Olympic Rain Forest, Sportster," she said. "We're heading home." Like the motorhome, I purred in response as we sped by the lush, green landscape. If cats were of the inclination to make favorites lists, the Olympic Forest campground would have made number one for me.

ACTIVATE LION MODE

We had been on the road for three months, traveling and experiencing the wild. Every day, we arrived at a new campsite, Judy watched my back while I explored. With coffee in one hand and my leash in the other, she became engrossed with my investigation of every leaf, bush and tree. When she tired, I accompanied her back to her fold up lawn chair in which she relaxed in the sunshine with a book. She idly scratched my ears as I stretched out beside her

She read and napped and I studied birds in the treetops and leaves whirling in the breeze. When the sun sank low in the sky, the rays backlighting the trees, shadows stretched out like a bunch of long tailed cats. It was then the forest came alive. Moths flitted above my head and rustling bushes sent thrilling shivers through me, but it was at that time Judy announced, "Time to go inside, Sportster. Time for dinner."

I plopped to the ground, refusing to move, but she tugged on my leash. I mewed in protest. A bird in a tree laughed at me.

Judy scolded with another tug on my leash. "Come on. It will be dark soon," she said. "There are boogie creatures in the night that will get you. You can't stay outside by yourself."

I scoffed at her warnings. Hadn't I been prowling all day? I had activated lion mode. I had sniffed the wild scents, yet not one of those "boogie creatures" dared to come out of their hiding. I had crouched by one of their holes for over an hour, and nothing. I was king of the forest. But not willing to create an embarrassing power struggle in front of the forest's residents, I acceded and allowed Judy to escort me inside to our warm, secure sanctuary. My day ended snuggled beside her as we watched TV.

I spent days in the Olympic Forest, prowling beneath the ferns. The pine-needled carpet felt as soft as a cat's paw, stirring deep yearnings inside me. Strange scents fed my active imagination. I dreamed of roaming as my feline ancestors had, in search of a graceful female to satisfy my every whim. Wasn't that how I was born to live? I loved my life with Judy. My home on wheels provided me with everything, a deep luxurious rug and my very own tiger-striped, cushy bed. But the forest's wild and seductive calls were bewitching, promising adventure and freedom.

Those thoughts were far from my mind now. Trembling, I crouched where I landed and attempted to gather my senses. Through the trees, I studied the grotesque scene. The vehicle's wheels spun in the air, and vapor hissed from its hood. An occasional ping disturbed the forest's eerie silence. My nosed twitched as a blade of grass tickled my nose.

Judy was nowhere in sight. I was in no mood to play the hide and seek game. She was never able to compete against my disappearing acts. Our mansion in southern California afforded curtains, chairs and couches to lurk behind, and shelves and dressers to perch upon. Tiptoeing into a room, Judy searched for me. I would pounce from a curtained lair, or refrigerator cliff, always the victor. She jumped and yelled in surprise. The game was great practice for when my dream of living in the wild came true. But if she was hiding now, I was not amused.

The sun sank below the treetops and darkness seeped into the forest. Hunger nagged at my belly. My eyes, still swelled large with adrenaline, scanned the area repeatedly. My tail twitched continuously. A baby meow squeaked past my tight throat. I hoped the forest muffled my feeble cry as it had my warrior's shout. This was no time to play the kitten's role.

From my covert position in the pines, the motorhome's shadow stretched from the road's edge and into a deep ditch. I don't know how much time had passed before I finally stood on all four shaky legs.

Nothing had changed in the forest. I gathered my lion's courage. The ferns draped as they had yesterday, luring me to prowl beneath them, to hunt for adventure. I peered up at the trees, which I longed to climb only a day before. They remained warm, wrapped in their cloaks of moss. Shadows hovered under the fern's fronds, which earlier had glistened and swayed in the sunlight. Nothing had changed, and yet, I sensed, without Judy, nothing would ever be the same. Wary of the deceiving quiet, I dared a step, then another.

I found her lying in the grass near the broken motorhome. An alarming metallic smell from a dark puddle beside her combined with her soft lavender scent and frightened me. Her heartbeat thumped erratically. I gently touched her face with a trembling paw and waited. Like a feather, I touched her again. Nothing.

Sirens, faint in the distance, gave me pause, their volume increasing as they neared. I took one, last look at

Judy's sleeping face and retreated, slinking back deeper into the forest. I hid in a rotted log. The alarms grew insistent, until their penetrating shrieks stabbed my ears and I blinked from the pain, almost crying out. Two trucks rushed up, braked, and their tires crunched off onto the roadside. The deafening din ceased, yet I remained crouched in the safety of the stump.

Beating off the invading night shadows, the fiery, flashing lights invaded my covert position and Illuminated the red maple leaves. Slamming doors and the strangers' shouts sent me shrinking even farther into the bowels of my fallen log.

Two men yanked open the back doors of their vehicle and jerked out a bed on wheels. Pushing it, they rushed to Judy's sleeping form and knelt down beside her. They hovered over her body, mumbling words to each other, and finally, lifted her up. They placed her on white sheets that glowed like the moonlight. Her body jiggled as they rolled her away and shoved her into the van. One of the men climbed in with Judy and the other jumped into the cab. In seconds, the sirens screamed again, and the van sped off, its shrieks fading as it raced down the road.

My heart pounded. They took my Judy! Panic and fury urged me to chase after the thieves. I started, but the kidnappers had already disappeared around the bend.

Anyway, clanging, banging sounds forced me to check my advance and I squeezed back even further into the stump. The other truck eased up to the motorhome. The passenger exited and stood behind my home, waving and shouting at the driver. After a series of rattles and clatter, the first man hooked the motorhome to a heavy chain leash and then disappeared back into the vehicle. The truck crawled back onto the asphalt and the motorhome followed.

My bag of food remained in the kitchen cabinet - my own private bathroom - my catnip mouse hidden under the passenger seat, and my treats - and my Judy – the hijackers took it all. The vehicle's light show drifted down the highway and it, too, vanished into the night. Once more, stillness took over the rain forest. Only an occasional vehicle swished past.

Judy was gone. My home was gone. This was not a game. This was not an "I'll see you later, Sportster." She was gone, like yesterday. My naptime passed, but still I waited. Feeling invisible under the log, I licked my paws, my tail and washed my face while the birds chirped their nighttime prayers.

Carried by the evening breeze, a strong, unfamiliar scent floated up my nose. With faltering steps, I crept out from under my hiding place, craned my neck, and raised up on my hind legs. A large animal, almost as big as my home on wheels, emerged from the depths of the forest with his head held high as the treetops. Overlooking me, he pranced by on a narrow path. His heavy odor stung my eyes. I tucked my tail under my trembling body and dashed back into my den. As quickly as the boogie monster had appeared, it vanished.

Shadows crept along the forest floor, tamping out the sun's invasion. The flaming maples cooled to grey and the green pines melted to black. I shivered. The moths and insects I enjoyed chasing yesterday flitted and danced in the chilling light. They taunted me, as if they knew I did not belong. Complete darkness overcame my new world, bringing with it an even more intense stillness.

The shelter of night stirred a fragment of courage within me, enough to venture out from my hiding. With each cautious step I paused, listened, and sniffed.

My eyesight, sharpest at night, allowed me to peer past the forest's edge. There in the grass lay Judy's sweatshirt, the one I snuggled upon when she left it on her bed. Finding me curled up in its fleece, Judy pushed her sweet smelling face into my fur, making sputtering noises that tickled my tummy. In response, I jumped up and walked away so she would not grow accustomed to my bewitching charm.

My heart fluttered at the memory and, forgetting my caution, I sprinted over to the garment. Inhaling her scent, visions of good times warmed me. I recalled watching nature shows on TV with Judy. They nurtured my dreams of living in the wild. They activated my lion mode and I imagined stalking the prey that crept across the TV screen. I thought of Judy working at her computer. I traced the mouse's trail with my paw, as it raced across her monitor. Memories of her laughter when I batted my catnip ball across the room made me happy. I chased after it, skidding around, grabbing the toy, and then swatted it back to her. All good practice for when I would ultimately live my "in the wild" dream. Was the time now?

ACTIVATE LION MODE

I nestled into her fleece jacket. My eyes scanned the expanse between the line of trees and the road I choked back a whimper. This was no game. A feeling of desperation, which I never experienced, pushed at me. I rose from Judy's sweatshirt and crept into the clearing. Every shaky step my courage diminished.

A path of sprinkled kibble led to my overturned water bowl and food dishes. My stomach growled. Ravenous, I crunched down a few kernels, but the chunks landed like rocks in my belly. My rhinestone collar hung on a nearby bush. Like glitter on a Christmas tree, the garnets caught the moonlight and my gold ID tag glowed. It must have been ripped off when I had been flung from the motorhome. No matter, it had always been a bother.

The kidnapper's scents rose from the deep gashes slashed in the damp earth by the motorhome's last journey, and Judy's scent, from where she had lain. Perhaps my eyes deceived me, and the pirates had not stolen off into the night with her. Perhaps I had been careless. I circled one last time, reexamining the scattered pieces of the motorhome - glass from the headlight, a towel, and a map -- scraps from our lives.I returned to Judy's sweatshirt and collapsed. My eyes drooped though I struggled to remain vigilant.

The new day stung with disappointment as daylight threaded through the woods, threatening to reveal my position. I was still alone. Making one more sweep of my surroundings, I listened for any familiar sound, and analyzed all the scents. No Judy.

I slipped back into the woods. I would wait.

~~JUDY HOWARD~~ SPORTSTER THE CAT

CHAPTER TWO

Many of the creatures in the woods lived a nocturnal life. Instead of rising with the sun, the creatures returned to their burrows, nests, or decayed logs after a night of hunting. I had tried to establish a similar routine at home, but Judy always squelched my idea. Well, she was not here now and this lifestyle would suit me. I retreated to my, now familiar, rotted trunk and crouched within its caverns. It had been a long night with little sleep. I stared at the bugs crawling on the stump's walls. The insects burrowed along self-made tunnels, content to ignore me. Unsure of my tenants, I blinked to stay awake.

****

The day crept on, dragging afternoon shadows and the humid air into my lair. Thoughts of Judy's steamy bathroom, and my love to drink from the faucet came to mind and I licked my dry lips. Rarely did I partake of the water from my bowl, preferring the fresh running water, which was, not only sweeter, but the rivulets intriguing. After I sated my thirst, I studied the wriggling patterns as they disappeared down the drain. I longed to watch the streams for hours, but Judy warned me, "If you don't drink, I turn it off." At first, I chuckled. Then she counted, "One. Two…." On the count of three, I learned she was serious. I waited until just before she said, "Three," and then I lapped up the cool liquid.

Licking my dry lips again, I swallowed hard. There was no water bowl in the woods, and no running faucets. Again, I thought of Judy. Would they bring her back? She had never stayed out all night.

Miffed, I planned a cool reception for her return. Finally, I rose, arched my back, and stretched until my elbows touched the ground and my tail dusted the log cave's ceiling. A butterfly fluttered by while I sat, contemplating my situation. Only yesterday, I would have bounded after the distraction without a care. Instead, I cleaned my fur. Just because I am living in the wild, is no reason to be lax in personal hygiene. As I bathed, I considered my options.

You have always wanted to live in the wild. Here's your chance. *You're hungry. What're you going to eat?* You've longed to sniff under every bush and prowl over every path, it's been your dream. *Where's the bathroom?* Your toes have twitched at the thought of chasing bugs, leaping at birds, or sleeping all day long. You're free. *What about food? What if Judy never comes back?*

Leaves rustled and played in the wind across the path and a strange scent permeated the spruce. Their branches crackled, shivered, and parted. My hair stood on end and I arched my back. I activated lion mode, emitted a low growl and froze. A huge ball of fur, Judy called them black bear, burst from the bushes onto the trail. His nose, ears, and hair resembling burly dogs I have known. I screamed with feline fury, but this creature was fatter, smellier, and wilder than any dog I had ever known.

ACTIVATE LION MODE

The bear rose up and became higher than the trees. His mouth gaped open, exposing his bright pink tongue embedded between razor teeth. He roared back at me and my stump dwelling vibrated. The breeze carried the animal's rancid breath to my nose. I sneezed. He locked his small black eyes on me. My city cat wisdom quickly sized up the situation. This wild, fat, smelly predator could crush my log home with one swipe of its cumbersome clawed foot. Swift reaction is a cat's best defense. I ran.

My panicked route snaked through the Spruce and Hemlock. At every turn, I lunged from the path to hide, imagining the black-eyed predator emerging from the sidelines. Then I regrouped and continued my flight. I pressed my ears flat against my head avoiding the branches raking against my ears. I didn't stop until my lungs begged for air. Squeezing beneath a root system growing above ground, I hunkered under its canopy and panted from fear.

Quivering, I caught my breath. My breathing slowed. Reassured I had out run the bear, I crept out and climbed up on the tree's runners. The scent of water made my dry mouth salivate. Like walking a tight rope, I balanced on top of the root system and followed the spreading tendrils toward the music of gurgling water. A stream rippled and bubbled and I jumped off my boardwalk onto a sandy beach.

My own endless running faucet! Approaching the water's edge, leaned over and lapped the clear, icy liquid, sweeter than any water I had ever drunk. I didn't stop until my belly bulged. Sated, I stepped back and sat down. Lifting one paw, I shook off the sand and licked it clean. Finishing, I repeated the ritual for my other feet.

I looked over my shoulder. The black bear was far behind, but he made my decision easy. I could not wait for Judy to come to me. I would simply head home. We would meet there. I growled, no longer just a little miffed. I hissed at a beetle who waved his antennae and crawled over my foot. Shaking off the warm images of home and Judy's comforting caresses that now constantly haunted me, I rose to begin my trek.

A movement in the creek drew my attention and I stared into the water's depth. A small school of tadpoles swerved back and forth, making their way downstream. I dipped my paw into the icy wetness to snare one, but with no claws, they slipped away. Another group approached, swimming within my reach. This time I grabbed faster and quicker. I cupped my paw and batted the little creature, like my ball, onto the creek bank. He twisted and flopped until I covered him with my foot and pinned him down. Living in the wild was not so hard. My tail twitched in anticipation of a meal and my belly rumbled.

The little guy's body quivered under my touch. I recalled my same response to the bear. I sniffed the little fish. He emitted an exotic flavor, in contrast to my kibble. My raging appetite urged me to make him my lunch. Exotic I am, but sushi is not my style. I lifted my paw and nudged my little captive toward the water's edge. He maneuvered a couple of flips and twists and splashed back into the cool depths. Like a bullet, he squiggled out of sight in search of his schoolmates. A tickly sensation tweaked within my chest as I pictured the little swimmer merging with his group. The same tingle occurred in the mornings at home, when I sat alongside Judy and tapped her face to awaken her. Every time, for as long as I could remember, she would open her eyes and purr my name. "Morning, Sportster." Every day, except yesterday.

    I shook off the memory. I'm burning daylight. How often had Judy said that? I shook to rid me of the sadness. It was best not to think of the past. My heart hurt when I reminisced, and my tummy ache was not letting up.

    My eyes followed the water's movement as various scents drifted over the water dotted by floating leaves. The stream flowed in the direction I needed to travel, to a place where the air was dry and trees were sparse. I lapped up one more long drink and turned away from the stream's edge. Wandered over to a small clearing, I could not hold out any longer. I wished for the privacy of my own bathroom as I pawed at the ground, cleaning away a spot, and squatted. Finishing, I worked quickly to cover my business and walked back to the brook. Searching my surroundings one last time, I rotated my ears up and down. With a deep breath, I switched my tail and headed down the path leading home.

    I traveled until a thorn pricked my foot. Stopping, I turned my paw, and examined it. The pad was bright pink with soreness. I dug at the needle with my teeth, but it only hurt more. Large droplets plopped upon my nose. They beat upon my ears and head and distracted me. I ignored the pain in my paw and tried to shake off the beads of water as if they were pesky flies. Their onslaught increased. Soon, not only was I drenched, but also the path had become a sea of mud. I sprinted for cover.

The downpour created tiny streams squiggling down a path, which traced along the creek, which now churned with muddy water. The raindrops hammered and then danced on leaves, springing to lower fronds, and then dripping down and disappearing into the rich black earth. Until now, I had only observed rainstorms from behind the motorhome's windshield. From that dry, safe interior, I marveled at the wriggling worms of water, scurrying across the glass. Now, I lived in the wild. Although chilly and wet, the experience excited me.

When the rain stopped, I ventured from my enclosure, another rotten log. Wet vegetation drooped heavily around me. I resumed my trek with increasing urgency, because now, not only my tummy ached from a hollow sensation, but also my foot burned like fire. Evaluating my route, I paused. The stream and the trail I followed turned abruptly to my right. I had grown comfortable with that path, but the way, which led home to Judy, veered to the left.

I trotted over to the graveled bank of the creek, which had swollen into a river. With nightfall approaching, the forest again was coming alive with its nocturnal residents. My muscles burned with a tiredness, which I had never experienced. Hunger pushed me to hunt for dinner but exhaustion held me back with a stronger force and won. I picked out a room for the night, for a change under a fallen log, which offered a view of the fast running river. Through the slits of my heavy eyelids, salmon, swimming upstream, performed pirouettes along a waterfall. My mouth watered. Perhaps tomorrow I would have fish for breakfast. There was something to say for living in the wild. No more dry, monotonous kibble.

***

Warmed by the morning sun, I sat up and climbed up on my "room's" roof. Atop the log, I performed what Judy had always called my yoga stretches. Dragonflies and butterflies swarmed above the water with the splashing salmon who had their own travel urgency. Although hungry, wading out into the cold rapids made the fishing solution seem less appealing. Maybe I didn't have far to go. I would wait for kibble.

My body ached from yesterday's trek and when my foot touched the ground, pain shot up my leg. Still, I performed my morning duties, and then filled my belly with more cold, sweet water. Taking a deep breath, I started off, steeled with determination to reach home before dark.

CHAPTER THREE

As the familiar path beside the river veered into the salty breeze to my right, I reluctantly turned away, limping down the less traveled track, which headed home. The night's rest relieved the soreness in my foot and my long drink abated my hunger. I felt good. Adventure! My tail twitched with excitement. With the bear and other boogie animal behind me, I looked forward to enjoying the wild the way I always imagined.

A sudden buzz sent my hackles up and I leaped into the air. The gossamer wings of a grasshopper jetted across the path, flicking against my nose. I landed, shaking off my foolish reaction. My green attacker rested quietly on a leaf and I pounced, pinning his green quivering body in my grasp. My tail vibrated from the thrill. I lifted my paw, curious, to take a closer look. He snatched the opportunity, soared high into the air and disappeared. For his small size, he was smart and swift.

Other bugs made me pause, but I meandered along, and the morning passed. Carrying my tail straight, I purred in contentment. The pride of living wild overrode my hunger and throbbing paw. I was free.

Soon I tired of the afternoon humidity and could no longer ignore my stomach's grumbling. My limp increased, and I stumbled. Collapsing in the middle of the path, I worked on my wound, licking and digging for the thorn.

Voices in the distance floated to my ears. The familiar aroma of barbequing drifted in the wind. Food? Could it be Judy? I stood, enduring my foot's pain, and resumed a steady pace, peeping little chirps of anticipation. I knew Judy could not have gone far.

The sounds and smells led me to the edge of a clearing. I halted. A brawny, grimy pit bull lay on the ground between a campfire and a small tent-like canopy. Picking up my scent, he raised his head and barked at my intrusion. Then springing from his prone position, he lunged at me but before I could assess the situation.

I dashed back toward the safety of the forest, but not before the jawbreaker added me to his blacklist. He crashed through the foliage and gave pursuit, close on my tail. I did not let my sore paw slow me down. Instinct and experience taught me how to deal with every bumbling move a dog could make. I left the frantic soul sniffing the path like a shop vat sucking dirt.

I perched high on a redwood stump protruding high from the forest floor. I licked my paws and washed my face, enjoying the moment. The fool dog sniffed through the foliage beneath me, never thinking to look up. A shout pierced the air. Jawbreaker raised his head, did an about turn, and bounded back to the clearing. I jumped down, padding behind him, as far as the wood's edge.

The dog loped back to a blue tarp, stretched over tree limbs and draped to the ground, creating a makeshift enclosure. Cozy, but not the kind of camping I am accustomed. Two plastic jugs, the tops cut off, sat alongside the tent-like structure. Jawbreaker's kibble was in one, his water in the other. My tummy rumbled.

A man with dark unkempt hair, whose only shirt was the ink from his tattoos, knelt down and patted the dog. Jawbreaker licked his face and danced with adoration. Dogs are so dependent. Jawbreaker would never make it one day alone in the rainforest.

Tattooman rose and approached the campfire, whose greasy blond curls snuck out from the confines of a knit cap and wound down around his bearded face. The other camper sat, six inches off the ground, on a stringy, webbed, aluminum lawn chair, next to a large plywood box. The fair-haired man's long legs spread wide, as he strummed a guitar. Tattooman shouted out to his camping friend. Guitarman parked the instrument against the pressed board wall of his home and stood. Grabbing a shiny plate resting on a nearby boulder, he strode over to the campfire and joined Tattoman and his dog.

"Somethin's in the woods." Tattooman said. "Did you see Pit take off?"

"Probably a raccoon or skunk," Guitarman said as he held out his shiny plate."You better hope it wasn't a skunk."

Tattoman took the plate. "I don't think so. Those varmints prowl at night..."

"Whatever it is, we're ready." Guitarman patted the leather casing on his belt that held a long knife.

"I don't think anyone's going to bother you, Yarborough-man." Tattooman's hand waved the air in front of his nose. "Jesus! It wouldn't matter if it was a skunk. Did the Green Berets forget to train you in proper hygiene?" He poked a pork chop with his less illustrious combat knife and plopped it on Guitarman's plate, an old hubcap.

The men devoured their meals, tossed the bones to the dog and wiped off their hubcap plates with handfuls of pine needles. Guitarman returned to his cardboard structure and his guitar while Tattooman stretched out on his own aluminum chaise lounge and picked up a book. I dozed, waiting for darkness to creep into the clearing.

When only the crickets, hoot owls and the campfire's crackle stirred the night, I stalked up to the clearing's edge. Moving from bush to bush and from small clumps of grass to another, I reached the blue tarp and crouched behind it. I waited, listening and smelling. Jawbreaker slept inside beside Tattooman on a makeshift cot. I sniffed for the kibble and crept forward. I drank first and then, surprised Jawbreaker had left his dish half-full, wolfed down the kibble. My crunching noise, the only sound echoing in the darkness.

Wakened by my scent and feeding frenzy, Jawbreaker rustled from under his covers. In an instant, he scrambled over his master's sleeping form and hit the ground running. I gulped down one more swallow of kibble and vaulted for the safety of the trees. I ran, airborne until pain shot through my tail and my retreat came to a sudden halt.

Twisting around, I found Jawbreaker's teeth clamped on my tail. Activate lion mode! I dug my back claws into his throat. Like butter, they sliced through the soft meat under his throat. I latched my front feet around his snout, sinking my teeth into his unprotected shiny black nose. I became the jawbreaker.

He jerked, yelping from the sting of my nails and the agony of my bite. Releasing me, he tossed me into the air. As the defeated Jawbreaker, yowled and rubbed his nose in the dirt, I landed on my feet, bolted across the clearing and vanished.

ACTIVATE LION MODE

CHAPTER FOUR

Stirring to the warmth of the morning's rays, I moved my tail gingerly and licked my injury. Only a scratch. I jumped down from my stump and proceeded toward Jawbreaker's camp. Everyone still slept. Again, I stole over to the kibble and water. I drank first, and then nibbled the few nuggets left in the bowl. Jawbreaker, wakened by the sound, raised his head. His nose, more bloody than black, twitched. Red streaks tracked down his neck, through his grimy hair, and disappeared between his legs. He started to rise, paused, and then only watched as I licked his bowl clean. As if looking for back up, he turned to Tatooman, who didn't move. I winked, enjoyed another long drink, and moseyed back to my perch in the forest.

Judy was not at this place, but my belly didn't ache anymore. Food and water would no longer be an issue. Settled on my stump high above the forest floor, I tended to my hygiene and meticulously cleaned my paw until the sky darkened and it began to rain, again. I sprang from my roost and ducked back into my familiar, hollow, rotten stump where I had spent the previous night.

The morning wore on, but so did the rain. Puddles oozed into my lair. I squeezed further into the recesses of the log to avoid the mud. No good. I waded out into the downpour. Heading back to the edge of the clearing, I studied the scene. The men stood around a large barrel wearing nothing as they massaged their skin with soap while nature's shower washed the suds away. Jawbreaker observed me from his blue-tarp-tent.

The pounding rain shrouded my approach as I ran toward the cardboard house and snuck inside. My movements, unnoticed by the men as they busied themselves with their showers. Jawbreaker decided to keep my operation covert. I shook off the excess moisture from my fur, found a blanket, and curled up. The rain beat a steady rhythm on the box, and I drifted into deep slumber.

****

The bed jiggled. Wondering why Judy was retiring so early, I purred and crawled next to her warmth. A strange scent filled my nostrils and my eyes sprang open. I leaped out of the covers. Guitarman also bolted upright, feet hitting the floor and slipping his knife from its sheath.

Back arched, I screamed my warrior call, froze and stood my ground. Face to face, armed to fight, we waited for the other to make the first move. Monitoring the situation, the man's face softened, his body shrank, and then mine. We both slowly let our hackles down.

"So you're the one responsible for last night's casualties to Pit." He sat down slowly onto a plastic milk crate in the corner and smiled at me. I jumped down from the cot and began to negotiate. I rubbed against his leg.

"The Green Berets trained me well, even gave me this Chris Reeves Yarborough knife at graduation." He ran his finger carefully along the blade's edge, then slipped the weapon into its case. "But they didn't teach me how to deal with these tactics." He reached down, and I went in for the kill. I sprang onto his lap, rolled on my back and exposed my belly.

He softened and rubbed my tummy. . His large hand trembled as he smoothed my soft fur. His lips formed a tight line and, his forehead knotted with emotional energy. I purred as loud as I could.

He carried me to the cot and we laid down together, me nuzzling his neck. He said no more as the rain pelted against the plywood roof throughout the rest of the day

Evening came with no letup in the storm. Guitarman rose and picked up the guitar. I listened to his music and studied his fingers dancing along the strings until Tattooman and Jawbreaker pulled back the rain soaked tarp and stepped inside. Discovering me on the bed, the dog barked in surprise and pressed close against his companion's leg.

"Well, what do you have there?" Tattooman sat down on a plastic crate.

"I'm holding this guy prisoner," Guitarman said. ". He's been stealing rations and is responsible for the attack on Pit yesterday." Guitarman nodded at the dog. "I see your dog doesn't feel any need for more interrogations."

"What're you gonna do with him? You gonna keep him?" Tattooman asked.

Guitarman scratched my head, and I leaned into his hand. "He's wet, and he has a sore paw."

Tattooman laughed. "I don't feel sorry for him. Look how he sliced up Pit's nose and neck."

Guitarman smiled proudly. "The cat's a warrior all right. He doesn't even have front claws. Can you believe it?"

"Buddhists believe that some souls are reborn as animals because of their past misdeeds. Maybe the cat was a Green Beret." The men nodded at one another.

I laughed at their serious philosophizing. Really? I'm a cat through and through.

"I think he's lost," Guitarman said. "When the rain let's up, I'll drive into town and look for posters. I don't have much hope though. By the looks of his sore feet, he's come a long way. If I keep him I'm going to name him Ka-Bar."

"When you get back from town, we're going to have to pack and move on. It's been nice for the summer, but this neck of the country gets as much as twelve feet of rain during the winter. So, unless you got a boat..."

Guitarman nodded. "We'll pack up and start heading south."

CHAPTER FIVE

On the second day of the storm, the veterans gave up waiting for the skies to clear. The cardboard sagged, heavy with rain, and the kibble bag, near empty, floated in a puddle. During those dim, dreary days, Tattooman and Jawbreaker dropped in and listened as Guitarman played his music. "I was at Gitmo," Guitarman said. "This rain forest takes me back. These nights aren't near as dark or as quiet, but the hair on my neck stands on end just thinking about it. " His hand slid over my back caressing me as he talked.

"Not me, I did Afghanistan. It wasn't like this. It was sand, sand, and more sand. Sand in your boots, sand in your eyes and sand in your teeth. When a dust storm blew, it reminded me of the blizzards back home in Illinois. We lost three men once on a mission during a haboob. I don't know about you, Bro, but this is better."

Tattooman leaned back, his arm around Jawbreaker. "I'll be glad to get out of here. Stirs up too many memories."

The hours passed as Guitarman strummed his guitar and they continued their grisly tales. Tattooman beat his chest with his Green Beret glory stories. The cardboard box shook from their fist pounding bull sessions. At the peak of these heart to hearts, Jawbreaker placed his front paws across Tattooman's lap. I followed the dog's lead by purring and head butting against Guitarman's leg.

*****

"Okay little guy, I mean Ka-Bar, you ride up front with the team." Guitarman picked me up and set me inside the truck's cab. He turned to Tattooman who surveyed the empty campsite and said, "All the gear's stashed and tarped in the truck bed." He motioned to the dog. "You too Pit, hop in." Jawbreaker jumped onto the seat, his agility remarkable for such a muscular dog. I took my place on the dash and occupied my time, studying the rivulets worming across the windshield while I considered my new macho name, Ka-Bar. I liked it. Jawbreaker licked his feet, cleaning them of mud. He must have picked up the cleanliness habit from me.

The truck rocked as Guitarman climbed in the driver's side. "Let's move 'em out," Turning the key, the engine sputtered and rumbled alive. "They say Portland is friendly to the homeless," Guitarman said." Check out the flyer on the dash. I picked it up at the shelter when I went to town."

Tattooman lifted my paw off the paper and slid the flier out from under me. "What's a Stand Down?"

"It's a huge event at the Portland fairgrounds this weekend. It's geared for homeless veterans. They're allowed to camp out and all kinds of services are provided. I'm going to get my driver's license renewed. They even have a veterinarian. You can get Pit's injuries looked at. I might have them look at Ka bar's paw, but it's looking a lot better. They'll have dentists, lawyers, and representatives from different colleges. There'll even be headhunters. Maybe we can find work. Either way, I figure we'll stay there 'til we decide what to do next."

Leaving tracks of mist behind, the freeway traffic crawled over the flooded asphalt like snails. The wipers beat a steady rhythm. I listened to the men's conversation and it became clear these men were strays, and not on a holiday, as I had thought earlier. I hoped they would find the assistance they needed at this Stand Down, because even from a cat's point of view, this was no way to live.

The rain decreased to a drizzle allowing some blue sky to appear as we pulled onto the fairgrounds. Covering the parking lot, a sea of bodies, duffle bags, tarps and canvas met us. Guitarman lowered his window when an official with an orange vest flagged us down.

"Find a spot anywhere." The man pointed. "Inside that building are volunteers to answer your questions and tell you where everything is."

"Thank you, Sir." Guitarman inched the truck to the edge of the lot of unfortunates who had strewn their meager possessions out, claiming their space on the asphalt. "This is as good a place as any." Putting the truck in park, he shut down the engine. "We'll spread out our stuff. Let it all dry out."

They opened the door and climbed out. I jumped to the ground followed by Jawbreaker. The dog and I prowled the fence line in search of a bit of dirt to serve as a bathroom. Tattooman approached while I was busy in the process of covering my business. "Pit, why don't you learn the little Ka-Bar's good habits?" He picked up the dog's residue, depositing it into a nearby trash container.

I followed them back to our spot in the parking lot. The openness left me feeling vulnerable so I took up surveillance under the truck. I estimated over a hundred bodies spanned the area. Many sat cross-legged staring off in the distance, while others paced up and down the make shift aisles. A loudspeaker blared out, announcing times of events and basic information. I caught the aroma of food just as the crowd must have. As a group, they rose from their small claimed spots and followed the scent.

My new Green Beret friends were no different. "Let's get some chow before it's all gone."

Guitarman squatted down, peering at me under the truck. "I'll see what I can bring back for you." I stepped out into the sunshine, showing my gratitude by rubbing up against him. He patted my back. "You wait here."

My eyes followed my travel companions until they became lost in the mass and disappeared into the building. I investigated their belongings laid out on the tarp, found the kibble bag, and busied myself chewing a hole in the side. I ate my fill as the kernels flowed out. Jawbreaker, who was becoming quite the gentleman, waited and then took my place when I left the table. He bellied up to the bag and consumed his share while I washed my face and paws.

Guitarman and Tattooman returned, both jacked up with excited energy. They clutched brochures and carried plastic bags bulging with more pamphlets. Guitarman sat down on the plastic crate." I'm excited about what the guy from the Portland P.D. said. If what he says is true, I'm going to apply." He leafed through a booklet. "He told me to go to the veteran's court and talk to a lawyer. They have the power to get my child support issues straightened out with the VA. And, they can arrange for me to get into a treatment program. Right away. In Philly there was a six-month waiting list. I told them, screw that. Completing the treatment program would get me cleared to apply at the academy. He said the Portland PD likes to hire vets."

"I have to admit, I'm pumped, too." Tattooman squatted beside Jawbreaker, scratching his ears. "I've got the apps for the Portland Community College and the State University. The VA even provides money for housing. We got here just in time. Classes start next week."

"And look here." Guitarman opened a bag of cat food and turned toward me. "I didn't have to sneak food. They gave me this."

I listened to the men's hopes and dreams. Yesterday they had been lost souls like me. Today, their spirits sprouted as if nourished by the rain. They had a long way to go. I realized that my journey, as well, was not as simple as I first thought. I considered Jawbreaker's position in this temporary family of mine. He belonged, I was the odd cat out. I swooned from a strong pang of homesickness. If I was going to make it home to Judy, I had to move on.

I ate my fill of fresh kibble, not knowing when I would eat again. My paws, no longer sore, felt calloused, and the minor scratch from Jawbreaker's overzealous attack had scabbed and fallen off. I hate goodbyes. I would leave at midnight.

CHAPTER SIX

The moon hung over the bodies and their scattered gear like a reading lamp. The starlight, dimmed from the city's lights, had lost its sparkle. For the amount of men and women strewn across the asphalt, the makeshift campground surprised me. The bustle had toned down to murmurs, occasional spurts of low laughter, and the sporadic bark of a dog. A good time to move out.

I studied my foster family one last time. Jawbreaker sensed something astir and lifted his head. I ignored his watchful eye, and headed out. When I looked back, he padded behind me, probably thinking I was taking a bathroom break. I stopped, jerked around, and hissed. His eyes widened, and heeding my warning, sat down. His big mouth drooped. I spun around and sprinted off into the night.

I jogged along the road. The city offered drainage ditches, underpasses, and an occasional abandoned building for hiding. Only two trucks passed.

Maintaining a steady pace, I made time. No sign of bears. No woodpeckers or hawks, but I jerked to a halt when I caught scent of an odor I had never experienced. Instinct told me it was not good. I froze and trembled. I wanted to run, return to my Green Beret friends and Jawbreaker, but chilling fear held me in place.

I recalled Judy pointing out the dead furry bodies along the roadside. "Do you see that, Sportster?" She'd say. "Bad things can happen if you aren't careful." She would shake her finger at me and say, "You have to stay close to home."

Well, I was not close to home, thanks to her, but I would be careful. I gathered my courage and followed the scent. On the edge of the road lay the ghastly carcass of a kitten. I belted out a yowl that pierced the night and I hightailed it. Careful, my tail! I didn't stop until my lungs begged for air and my legs screamed for relief. With a last burst of energy, I dove into a large pipe leading under the freeway. Rancid water splashed in my face as I sprinted toward the dim moonlight at the end of the tunnel. My stomach hurled, and I gagged from the offending stench, but I kept going. The passageway opened into a concrete ditch enclosed by cyclone fencing. Without slowing, I rushed the line of chain link and taking advantage of my momentum, I scrambled over the top. The ear-piercing rattle of the metal spurred me over the top and I leaped down on the other side. With the barrier between the crime scene, and me I stopped and caught my breath.

I had landed in another parking lot. A large Elk, his head held high, sporting a wide rack of horns stood in front of a building. I balked. My hair stood on end. Wait. It was only a statue. This was an Elks Lodge. Judy and I had camped at many of these facilities. Fraternities of a sort, their symbol, the Elk, guarded the lodge's entrance. I scanned the parking area. Several RVs nestled in the rear of the property. One looked like our motorhome.

My chest pounded with excitement, yet I crept along the brick wall that met the fencing. A longer, but a safer way to reach the vehicle, but I must be cautious. Like most campgrounds at night, all was quiet. My heart raced as I neared the motorhome. Judy had not made it easy for me to find her. She would be happy to see me. I imagined her reaction after six nights without me. She would feed me my favorite treats and kiss my face while I pretended irritation at her gushing. I purred with anticipation, and climbed onto the motorhome's porch.

When my paw touched the first step, my heart sank. This was not our home. Strangers' scents coated the porch and the door. My tail drooped. A heavy spirit weighed me down, accenting my exhaustion. I crawled onto the porch. Too tired to be careful, I curled up, tucked my nose under my flank and closed my eyes.

****

The warm morning sun lulled me awake along with the motorhome's rocking movement. I crawled off to a covert position under the vehicle. Voices inside mumbled until the door lock made a familiar click. Then a man spoke clearly. "There you go, Annabelle. Can't you let us sleep late just once?"

The door slammed shut as a soft ball of fur, glided down the steps. Grey paws reached out from Annabelle's plush body, carrying her to the ground. She performed her own yoga stretch, her elbows flat on the asphalt, and her butt in the air. She must have seen me because her tail gyrated, then kinked into a small hook at the tip, as if calling me.

I sprang to my feet and approached like an eager peep on twitter, chirping my intentions, my exhaustion forgotten. She turned and her icy blue eyes grew large. I chirped a more alluring trill this time. She stood her ground, but her tail flagged back and forth.

I presented myself, nose to nose, and suddenly became aware of my unkempt condition. My cologne was the rancid tunnel water from yesterday. My tail, erect and vibrating, exhibited a glaring bald spot from Jawbreaker's attack. I quickly lowered it before she noticed, rolled over, and showed her my soft underbelly … and the burrs embedded in my coat. I had been too fatigued last night to groom myself. Shame spurred me to jump up and dash away into the bushes.

CHAPTER SEVEN

Under the cover of the bushes, I looked her way. She stared, and I stared back. I wanted her to come to me. She sniffed the ground around her, as if I were of no concern to her, but her flagging tail gave her away.

Shameless of my frightful condition, I trotted back and sniffed her butt. I again, performed my dance. She purred her approval and rubbed up against me. My oil-slicked hair, heavy with stink excited her.

Her pink rhinestone necklace was wide with many rows of jewels. Polished nails matched her collar and the pink bow behind her ear.

She led me back to the motorhome and pranced up the steps. She sat in front of the door, switched her tail, and released a loud meow. I hesitated only a moment and then followed onto the steps, sitting down beside her. The door opened and she sprang inside. Where you go I go, baby. I slipped in as the door slammed shut.

"Annabelle, what have you brought home this time?" Annabelle ignored her caretaker and led me to her food dish. Embedded with gems, it, too, sparked like her eyes and her collar. I held back while she sniffed her empty bowl. She raised her gaze up to the man and belted out a meow. My heart flip-flopped, and my tail shivered.

"Okay Annabelle. I know you want breakfast. I suppose for your friend, too? We didn't teach you to be inhospitable."

Like a feather floating on a pond, Annabelle set her rear down in front of her dish. Another pang of desire shot up my tail. It quivered. Distracting me from the illusion before me, my stomach roared with hunger. The whir of a can opener carried the scent of tuna down to our noses. Annabelle pranced and twirled as the man bent down and spooned the contents into her dish. I rushed forward, shoved my newfound friend away and gobbled down the bountiful breakfast. The rich meal slid down my throat like the icy water from a stream.

My girlfriend's tiny meows spiked my ecstasy as I licked her fancy bowl clean. Annabelle paced around the kitchen, flicking her tail in distress. The whir of the can opener sounded again, and I imitated her hungry dance. More would be supreme.

The man picked up the empty dish, and setting it on the counter, scooped the contents from the can into the bowl. Annabelle was attracted to bad cats. I didn't have to be polite. I leaped onto the counter, shoved his hand away, and wolfed down the tuna.

"Oh no, little guy." He grabbed me, pulling me away.

ACTIVATE LION MODE

Little guy? I hissed, twisted, and sank my teeth in his arm. He bellowed, released me, and I dropped to the floor. Annabelle's eyes grew large, shifting from me to the man. She was afraid for me, yet she smiled. Now, I knew she liked bad boys. With her encouragement, I hissed and growled, strutting in circles around the small kitchen.

The man rolled up his sleeve and examined his injury. "Margaret. You're going to have to get up. Annabelle has brought in another one of her strays and he bit me."

Margaret emerged from under the covers in the bedroom, only two steps from the kitchen. "Who could sleep? Are you okay, has he had his shots?"

"I'm okay, but he doesn't have a collar, so no tags."

Everyone but Annabelle was upset. I reversed my tactics and attempted to manipulate the situation in my favor. I repeated apologetic meows and rubbed back and forth against the man's bare hairy leg.

Margaret scooted to the edge of the bed and slipped her pudgy feet into slippers. "Let me see, Stan."

Stan held out his arm and removed the bloody paper towel he used to dab the wound.

"I'm worried," Margaret said. "Cat bites can become ugly in a matter of hours. And we don't know if he's had his shots." She peered down at me as I fervently tried to make amends. "He's docile now. Why don't you put him in Annabelle's carrier until we figure out what to do?"

"Yes, I guess that's best." Stan bent down and picked me up. Assured my strategy had worked, I rubbed my head against his chest and purred even louder. He scratched my ears and before I realized his intentions, he shoved me in a cage and shut the door. What? I stared at him, then Margaret.

"Sorry, little guy." Stan hung his head and turned away. I overlooked the demeaning term of endearment. Now I had a bigger problem.

Judy *never* put me in a cage. Sure, I had a carrier, an imitation leather bag with a gold zipper, but she *never, never* zipped it up. I yowled.

Stan and Margaret scurried around in the small space of the motorhome, dressing and taking turns in the tiny bathroom. Annabelle came over, mewed her tiny meow, and laid down in front of the carrier's metal gate. She appeared downhearted until she moved to the couch, stretched out and went to sleep. I had myself in a dandy spot because of her, but I guess things could be worse.

******

They slung my carrier into the back seat of their tow vehicle parked in front of the motorhome. They didn't speak as they pulled onto the freeway and then Margaret said, "The shelter's the next exit."

The shelter? I know what a shelter is. I yowled with an upgraded, intense desperation. I could not go to the shelter. I'd heard stories. You don't come back from the shelter. They parked and opened the car door. The panicked cries of barking dogs and smell of death hung in the air. Things had just gotten worse.

~~JUDY HOWARD~~ SPORTSTER THE CAT

CHAPTER EIGHT

I roared and spit with every panicked breath. The man and woman did not respond. They entered the building, and carried me to a reception area.

"May I help you?" A young man, his head shaved and wearing scrubs, drew his attention from his paperwork.

"We have a stray here," Margaret said.

What? Stray? I'm not a stray!

"Our Annabelle brought him in off the street. She's always attracted to dirty male cats."

"I'M NOT A STRAY." I yowled. No one looked at me.

"He bit my husband when he tried to pick him up."

Okay, I tried to make up for that. I was just showing off for Annabelle. I see she didn't come along for this ride. I jerked my tail back and forth. It thumped against the carrier wall, matching my pounding heartbeat. I panted. I couldn't catch my breath. My stomach lurched and the tuna from breakfast slid up my throat. Gagging, I spit up a slimy glob and crouched in the corner of the cage, licking the slippery smelly goop from my paw.

ACTIVATE LION MODE

The man shoved some paperwork toward the elderly couple and said, "Sign here. I'll scan him for a chip and bring your carrier right back." The shaved head carried me through swinging doors and the barking increased ten decibels. The dogs' desperate voices echoed off the concrete walls and between the barks, soft meows whispered. He approached a large cage that reached to the ceiling. He set my carrier on a nearby table and opened my door. Finally, someone listened. I mewed, as he pulled me out. I mewed again, this time with relief. He rubbed my ears, and I pushed my head against his touch. Finally, someone cared. The kennel boy slipped a collar over my head, not a fancy one like my black rhinestone, but it was a beginning.

As he grabbed an instrument from the table, we both tensed to a roar of aggressive barking and shouts from the dog area. "Hey Jim! We need a hand here!" Jim threw the scanning instrument on the table, carried me to the huge cage and shoved me inside. "I'll scan you later. I hope we'll find a home for you, but I had to mark you down as a biter."

I didn't mean it. Doesn't anybody listen? It was an accident.

He locked the gate behind him, and rushed away. One more time despair spread through me. I lifted my gaze, scanning my surroundings. Shelves, like stair steps, climbed the cage walls. Cat eyes stared at me from every direction. I hung my head and huddled in the middle of the floor, there was nowhere to go. An ache crept through me, hurting from the inside out. On each shelf and every corner crouched a cat, each a different size, each a different color. They all stared at me. I growled and pretended to sniff the ground.

I dared to stand and pick my way, sniffing as I went, toward the sand box in the corner. A fluffy bed smelled like a thousand cats held a motley litter of sleeping kittens. How could they sleep? I climbed in the sand box, made my mark, and covered it.

As I stepped out, a female cat, who would have been white if not for the grease defacing her, crept up, one hesitant step at a time, toward me. A black male prowled close behind her as if to watch her back. Across his face and body, white blotches of blistered skin contrasted against his black swarthy fur. The scars proved as medals, ranking him king of the cage. He monitored every move I made. I had enough of conniving females, but I needed to know the score in this place. I ignored the black and let out a half chirp, half growl in greeting. She peeped an answer and covered the distance between us.

We touched noses, and then butts, as Blackie hung back, watching. Scars pocked her pink nose and her tummy hung loose. Scabs encrusted one ear and was absent its tip. If Blackie was her protector, he was not doing his job. She glanced at the king and cringed at his glare.

I turned and met his stare. My challenge sprang the tension, and he pounced, screaming his intention to cut me. His claws struck my cheek as I turned, whipped around and mounted him. My own back claws dug into his back, and I felt his skin rip as I sank my teeth deep into his neck. He shrieked. The brawl was over as quickly as it had begun. Blackie slunk to a corner.

Miss Not-So-Snow White had not moved. I turned my back on Blackie, rubbed against her, and she rolled over for me. I stepped away, stretched out in the center of the floor and scanned the inmates. Locking eyes with each one, each declined my challenge, and turned away. Miss Not So Snow White took her place beside me.

I noticed her belly, nearly bare and her teats swollen. She was no Annabelle, but I sensed Miss Not-So-Snow White would not sell me out after a romp in the grass.

The din of the inmates' barking had quieted, but now as a young couple entered the cell block, again climbed the to the top of the noise charts The frenzied barking pricked my nerves and I glanced at Miss Snow. She stood up and sauntered up to the chain link fencing that jailed us.

The couple responded to Miss-Not-So-White's friendliness. The woman, who wore tights and a long sweater, knelt down. "Oh Look at her, Richard. It looks like she's had kittens." Her finger poked through the fence and Miss Snow rubbed affectionately against it.

Richard crouched beside his girl. "The kennel boy said she had a litter of four, too young to be taken away. If we adopt her we have to take the kittens, too."

Miss Snow's demonstration showed me how it was done. I jumped in and followed her lead.

The girl turned her attention to me. "Look at this one. He's beautiful. We could call him Mittens. See his white paws?" She stuck her finger through the chain link and I pushed my head against it, showing my desperation.

Mittens? What kind of name is that for a cat who lives in the wild and who just earned the title, King Of The Cage? Miss Not-So-White left the fence line and climbed into the large bed in the corner. Her kittens crawled around her, nudging and mewing.

I turned back to Richard and the woman, now focused on me. "He's so sweet. What do you think?" The woman looked up at Richard, pleading.

I glanced back at Miss Snow, whose honor I had just defended. Engrossed in mothering, she licked her charges as they fed. I swung my attention back to my potential rescuers, hissed, spat, and slammed my mitten paws against the floor. I hunched my back, shot my tail up straight, and growled. The girl jumped back as Richard said, "Oh my! He's a wild one. I guess he's not so sweet."

ACTIVATE LION MODE

Walking away, I lay back down by Miss Snow and her family. Miss Snow needed a home. I sensed Richard and his girl would take on the responsibility. Miss Snow had shown me the ropes and now I knew how to get out of here, but this was Miss Snow's chance. Blackie sulked in the corner. I couldn't leave her with him.

CHAPTER NINE

Richard and the woman stood outside my cell and looked at one another. Glancing back at me, he girl's face reflected a hint of sadness. "You're right, Richard," she said, "No one's going to adopt a cat with kittens. What chance does she have?" The girl's sad eyes focused on me, this time watered with tears.

Richard wrapped his arm around the girl and steered her toward the reception area. "Come on. Let's go fill out the paper work." Her shoulders sagged and she hung her head as she wiped her eyes.

The dogs' barking ceased. Somewhere in the bowels of this prison, the metallic clank of a gate echoed off the cinder block walls. The couple disappeared though the door into the room where they altered pets' lives with the scratch of a pen. Miss Snow's blue cat eyes met mine. I returned her questioning gaze with a long blink of assurance, but she continued to study me until I turned away.

My gratitude to Miss Not so White embarrassed me. She had demonstrated how to play the 'adopt me' game, and win these strangers over. Although her purring blue eyes drew me in, her adoration made me uncomfortable. I remained in place, twitched my tail, and began licking my paw. Tomorrow was another day. I would play the "adopt me" game on the next rescuers, and then, once outside, escape. After all, now I had not only earned title of The King, but also the title The Wild One, too.

A kennel boy entered and scooped mounds of kibble into a half dozen dishes lining the fence line. The cell's population stirred, but waited, their focus on me. I stood and padded toward the food, their signal to scurry to the various other pans of food. Blackie skulked to the dish furthest from mine. By now, long shadows accompanied by a chill crept across the concrete. I ate my fill, satisfied my thirst, and settled down by Miss Snow and her family. My heavy eyelids drooped and I dozed. Exhaustion seeped in with the cold, penetrating my bones. I shivered. I would give anything to be snuggled by Judy's side.

The alarming ruckus of barking dogs' pulled me back from sweet dreams of home when the reception's door to freedom burst open. The kennel boy accompanied the girl. Richard clutched a handful of papers and lugged a large cage. The group chattered amongst one another and the girl beamed with excited energy. My heart sank. I wished I had shown my gratitude to Miss Snow, but now it was too late. We exchanged silent goodbyes.

ACTIVATE LION MODE

The gate clanked as it swung wide and everyone squeezed into the cell. "What are we going to name her?" The woman asked.

Richard stood back enjoying the pleasure on his wife's face. "How about Snow White?" he said. "Katie loves that story. We'll let her name the kittens."

Only then did I notice the woman's swollen belly. She reached down, scooped up a kitten, and cradled the wiggling form. "These guys will keep her busy when her new brother arrives." She propped the fur ball on the mound of her belly and caressed it. "She's going to be so surprised."

I remained near the big bed with Miss Snow and her litter. She was going to a good home and I was happy for her. My heart twisted with my own fond memories of Judy and me, the ache so strong, I released a long, loud meow. The woman looked over at me and smiled warmly. "Don't worry, Mittens. We're taking you too." She placed the kitten back in the bed and reached out to me.

Did I hear correctly? I hesitated then rubbed against her hand. "You didn't fool me, little guy," she said. "I know you wanted to help out your gal, here. I don't think you are really a biter." She scratched my ears. "I saw how you two looked at one another." She cupped my face in her palms. "That was a noble thing you did. It took some convincing, but the director of the shelter himself gave us the okay to adopt you. Of course we had to sign the proper release forms."

"Come on, Mellie, let's get them in the carrier." Richard set the large cage down and the kennel boy began placing the kittens inside.

Mellie slid her hand under my tummy and lifted me up. I do not tolerate strangers holding me, but she had earned the privilege. Thanks to Mellie, I was getting out of here.

Mellie handed me to the young man who pushed me into the cage, already crowded with Miss Snow and her mewing litter. Relief washed over me. It was true. I was adopted, too. I would have gone crazy wild if I had to remain any longer defending my top cat position. The future appeared brighter.

The long ride passed with comforting chatter between Richard and Mellie. The trees swished by, their leaves backlit by the setting sun. The sky melted from red to orange, and finally to shades of grey. The car crunched up a gravel drive. Richard parked and turned off the engine. "We're home," he said.

Richard and Mellie were prepared. They carried us to a room, set our carrier down, and opened the door. "Come on out you guys. Come see your new home." Mellie's face filled the cage's doorway as she lay on the floor and peered inside. "Come on."

I peeked out from the carrier's security and studied the surroundings. Stretching to the ceiling, a kitty condo high-rise stood in the corner of the room. Catnip wafted from the feathery things dangling from the various levels. Tucked beside a chair was a small pet bed. I glanced up at Mellie. "I know, Mittens. We need more sleeping quarters." She laughed. "We hadn't planned on adopting an entire family." Her giggles reminded me of Judy.

I glanced at Miss Snow and ventured the rest of the way out of the cage. From the safety of the enclosure, Miss Snow observed my investigation while I sniffed everything in the room. Full-length curtains draped to the floor waiting for the kittens to climb. A full sized bed made this a guest bedroom. A door led to a tiled bathroom and a litter box. I did my business and made my mark.

As I came out of the bathroom, Miss Snow hovered over her charges as she ventured into their new environment. I wondered if Miss Snow had ever lived like this. I guessed not. A cat can really get used to this kind of life. Living in the wild is not all I had dreamed it would be. After tracing my path around the room, Miss Snow steered her clan to the bed and they all climbed in. She laid down and her flock scurried to her. She licked each one as it nursed. Miss Snow would adapt well to her new life.

CHAPTER TEN

A small voice penetrated the closed door. "Where are they? Can I see them?" The door opened and a chair on wheels preceded Mellie and Richard as they entered.

Richard maneuvered the chair into the center of the room. "Okay, Katie. Which one would you like to hold first?"

Katie spotted Miss Snow and her wriggling litter. She let out a tiny squeal in accord with her frail body and clapped her hands. Neon colored tennis shoes blinked as they dangled, barely reaching the footrests. The pink and green headband failed to distract from the tragedy that Katie had no girly curls. She was bald. Still, she radiated a delight, which should have flushed her translucent complexion.

I remained beside Miss Snow and her litter as the delicate girl examined one of the kittens, which her mother presented to her.

"Let's see, there are four babies, right?" Katie twisted to catch her daddy's expression.

He nodded but remained by the door.

I sensed his reserve. He wore it like a coat in cold weather.

"So, four names, hmmm." She said and laid her small index finger against her sunken cheek. Studying the furry form wriggling in her lap she said, "This is a girl, right, Mom?"

Nodding, Mellie's warm smile radiated every wish a mother could want for her daughter.

"I'll name her Charlotte after my chemo nurse. This kitten has got blond hair like her."

A bolt of pain flashed in Mellie's eyes, but she leaned down and kissed Katie on her shiny head. "That's a sweet name, honey"

She exchanged the newly christened Charlotte with a small black ball of fur. "What about this guy? This is a boy. Look. His soft coat is like the velvety night sky."

"He's beautiful. Midnight. Let's call him Midnight. Because no matter how dark it is, the sky is still beautiful with all its twinkling stars." With a light pat on the head, Katie handed Midnight back to Mellie.

I admired the girl's moxie. Her spirit sparked, in contrast to the subdued emotions of her parents'. I sprinted across the room and jumped into Katie's lap. Purring, I rubbed against her boney chest. She squealed again, giggled, and wrapped her rail-thin arms around me.

Mellie laughed at her daughter's response. "That's Mittens. See how he has white mittens on his paws?"

Katie's feather fingers brushed against my toes, and I nudged my head under her pinky. Her digits fluttered over my nose and scratched my ears. Katie's energy waned as her mother held up another kitten.

Katie pointed to the orange and black squirming form in Mellie's arms. "That one reminds me of Destiny. Remember her, mom?"

Again, a flash of distress. "I do, honey. She's with the angels now."

"Yes, but I talk to her all the time. She's my best friend." Katie reached up and caressed the black and orange kitten. "This one's brave. See how she looks me right in the eye? Destiny was like that. She wasn't afraid of anything." Katie's birdlike hands traced over me, and I curled up in her lap. She looked back to her father. "I'm getting tired, now. I think I should go lay down. Can I name the last one later?"

Her father's attempt to smile turned into a grimace. "Sure, honey." He met his wife's gaze, as if to draw from her strength.

"Can Mittens sleep with me? He needs a nap, too."

Both parents studied me and traded shrugs. Relief flooded over me. Not that I didn't want to stay with Miss Snow and play daddy to a bunch of mewing youngsters, but I sensed an urgency to be with Katie.

I surveyed the layout of the house as I rode on Katie's lap down the hall, making note of the doors, one in the living room and the other off the kitchen. Ruffles and stuffed animals decorated Katie's room. Richard wheeled us next to the bed. He bent down to lift his brave daughter out of the chair and into the canopied bed. Her undernourished arm shot out, pushing him away. "I can do it," she said. I leaped onto the covers when she stood. Her toothpick legs poked in her blinking tennis shoes, wobbled to support her, yet she leaned against the bed and laughed at me. "I wish I could jump like that. I need a boost. " Dad jumped forward, his big hands encircled her waist and lifted her up. She crawled up to her pillows and almost disappeared into their plushness. I took my place by her side. "Mittens will go with me to dreamland." She cradled me as I snuggled up and went to sleep.

I awoke in the early morning hours when Destiny came for her best friend. Katie's spirit floated around me, and I felt her kindness and gratitude brush across my fur. She kissed me on the head and thanked me for staying. "Tell Mom and Dad I love them, will you, Mittens?" Her good bye lingered like a song in the darkness and then she floated away.

When her body grew cold, I left her and prowled through the house. Miss Snow's door remained closed so I made my way to the master bedroom. I jumped into the king-size bed and cuddled up to Mellie, whose legs and arms wrapped tightly around her husband's. I studied her face, her features slack in worry-free slumber. I touched her lightly with my paw. She needed to know her Katie was gone.

ACTIVATE LION MODE

CHAPTER ELEVEN

Mellie's eyelids flickered open. Her face registered surprise and then only a moment of delight until her mind recognized me. I watched her brain deduce my reason for waking her and her eyes widened. They flashed with the familiar despair that lived in their dark brown shadows. She reached from under the covers and slid her hand over my body. Her scent reminded me of the jasmine that decorated our porch at home with serenity. There would be no tranquility for Mellie today. She rolled over to look at her husband. With a feathery touch, she traced her finger across his morning whiskers, careful not to wake him. Slipping out from under his arm, she scooted to the edge and paused. Taking a deep breath, her mouth set in a thin line. She squared her shoulders and rose.

I padded past her and peered into Katie's room. In the corner a gossamer image of Katie held the hand of her little friend she had called Destiny. "Hi, Mittens," Katie said, and turned to her big-eyed friend. "Destiny, this is my new friend, Mittens."

Mellie paused at the door with me and shivered as she studied Katie, enveloped in the ample bedcovers. I pushed past her, jumped onto the bed, and took my vigil alongside Katie's lifeless form. Tears swelled in Mellie's eyes as she gazed at her daughter's still body. Katie burst forward in a gust of warm air and wrapped her arms around her mother's legs. She pressed her unearthly body against her mother and said, "Don't worry, mom. I'm with Destiny now. I'm fine." Mellie blinked and shivered from the draft encircling her bare legs. With her palms, she wiped the tears flowing down her ashen cheeks and approached her daughter's still body. Leaning down, she kissed her daughter's forehead. Her hand trembled as she smoothed her little girl's temple, as if the child's boisterous curls still remained.

"Oh, Katie, I thought maybe you would have stayed long enough to meet your new brother." Mellie looked at me. "You knew, didn't you?" She picked me up and cradled me, rocking back and forth, as she probably had done for Katie as a baby. She buried her face in my fur. Her body shook as she sobbed while I rubbed my cheek against hers. "Thank you Mittens, for staying with her." She rocked, and I purred as the morning pushed through the sheer curtains. I surveyed the room. Katie and her friend were gone.

Richard's footfall sounded in the hall. He, too, paused at the doorway. Unnoticed by his wife, he watched us. The heavy sadness pulled his shoulders down. His jaw tightened, flexing the muscles in his neck. He inhaled deeply, stepped up behind Mellie and embraced her. The three of us rocked back and forth while Mellie hummed a lullaby.

I wished Katie had waited for her father before she left. His arms slackened and he leaned in and kissed Mellie. His hand smoothed over my head and under my chin, lifting it up so our eyes met. "Mittens." Like his wife's, his eyes filled with tears, too. I pressed against his palm and he hugged us tightly. Finally, he raised up and focused on his daughter's still form. Leaning over, his lips brushed her cool forehead.

"You will always be daddy's girl," he said and pulled the bedcovers over her thin body. He turned back to Mellie and me. "She's free now. No more battles to fight." He reached an arm around his wife. A comforting energy passed between them.

They left Katie and moved to the kitchen. I followed and found an unobtrusive spot near the door leading to the garage. Richard sat at a small desk with a computer and phone. "I'll call our folks first, before the hospice nurse."

Mellie, her back to Richard, fumbled with two coffee mugs as she poured steaming coffee from the automatic pot as it burped out its last squirt of caffeine. She returned the carafe to the hot plate. Her body tensed. She slammed her palms on the countertop, hung her head and leaned against the counter. Her shoulders shook uncontrollably with each deep sobbing moan. Richard jumped up and rushed to her.

"I'm okay." Wiping her nose with a napkin, she pulled away. "I'm going to check on Snow and her kittens."

When she opened the door, I sprinted into the room. Miss Snow, now christened as Snow, perched on a ledge of the condo, observing her charges, who rolled and romped on the area rug below. I crossed the space, jumped up, and joined Snow on her shelf. We sniffed one another. Her ice blue eyes widened as she picked up Katie's scent.

Mellie finished an examination of each kitten with a kiss on its head and then approached Snow and me. She reached up, scratched behind Snow's ears and said, "Did you know your Mittens here did a brave thing last night?" Snow purred loudly in response. Mellie looked at me and added, "Mittens is a good friend." She patted my head, turned, and picked up the food and water dishes. I slipped between her legs as she exited the bedroom, dashed down the hall, and resumed my vigil by Katie's body.

The lonely morning transformed into a hustle of people arriving and leaving. As visitors paid their respects to Katie, I remained steadfast by her side until strangers lifted her onto a bed with wheels like the one on which they carried Judy away. I jumped down, and followed them to the front door. While everyone said their last good byes to Katie, I sneaked outside and took cover in the bushes.

Richard and Mellie huddled on the porch as the van transporting Katie disappeared down the road. The couple held one another. They didn't cry, but their heavy sadness hung in the air. I felt their oneness, too, and knew they were going to survive this. They had each other ...and a new life on the way.

~~JUDY HOWARD~~ SPORTSTER THE CAT

CHAPTER TWELVE

I turned my face to the breeze. Its whispering sigh and reminded me of my freedom. I remembered my dreams, how my tail twitched, perched on the windowsill. How many hours of my life had I chirped at the sparrows who, unconcerned by my presence on the other side of the glass, hopped beyond my reach, pecking at a string of ants? I studied Larry the lizard bopping his head to hypnotize his prey and basking in the afternoon rays on our patio at home. I remembered the one wish I had wished - for the feline gods to grant me – to be free.

I peeked through the bushes at Mellie and Richard holding hands as they shuffled into the house. The door closed securely with a click. How long had my journey been up to this point? I didn't know. It seemed like forever. The ache for Judy had only grown stronger and instinct told me I was nowhere near home.

But today my belly was full and my paws healed. I leaped up, swatted a fly, and pounced on a beetle trudging through the rotting foliage. A startled bird, hiding on a branch, shrieked, flapped his wings and pounded the air, escaping in flight. I jumped in surprise, hissed my lion warning at him and then sprinted toward a grassy area across the street. My paws touched the warm asphalt as a truck, roared at me from out of nowhere. No time to call upon the cat gods, I grabbed a deep breath, pointed my tail skyward, and lurched for the sidewalk. Exhaust fumes swirled from the vehicle's wake, choking me, but I sailed over the sidewalk, and my feet landed on the soft, cool, green grass. Spitting and sneezing, my tail pointed skyward, I bolted under a picnic table shaded by a large oak tree. Crouching under its protection, I gathered my senses as I cleaned my fur of the oily smog. At times, I paused from my duties and studied the park's population. Two mothers sat on a bench by the swing sets and jungle bars. Each absently rocked their strollers as they focused on the sandy play area. Five children, ranging from small tots digging in the sand box, to an older boy, dangling from the jungle gym, squealed and yelled. Their giggles and garbled voices mixed with an occasional reprimand from one of the mothers.

I could still see Mellie and Richard's house across the street. I wondered how often Katie had played here. I thought of going back, but Richard and Mellie had each other. Everyone seemed to belong to someone, like I had belonged to Judy. I wouldn't fit in.

My eyelids grew heavy. The afternoon shadows grew long. Thoughts and visions floated in and out, as I napped.

Annabelle's fluffy image came to mind and my tail shivered. Her alluring, plush life had been intoxicating. My mouth watered, as I tasted the memory of her tuna casserole. I had overlooked her love handles hidden under her soft, sweet smelling fur. Would I have fit into her rhinestone life? Annabelle's ribbons and stones were not my style, and anyway Annabelle's life was lacking. Her only excitement occurred when she took in an occasional stray, who was sure to enjoy the comforts she offered. But a vagabond cat is drawn to a life of roaming, just as much as Annabelle was attracted to him. His love of freedom would eventually stir up a restlessness and lure him to chase the scents in the wind. He would become bored with her company and move on. Being free, that is what Annabelle's life lacked.

Freedom is seductive. I learned this firsthand from a yellow cat I called Top Cat. Last year the mangy orange tabby roamed my neighborhood back home, often shadowing my door in the middle of the night. He stalked me, taunted me, and threatened to take over my territory, as limited as it was. He jeered at my jeweled collar. I hated him, yet envied his life. I burned with jealousy of his abilities. Worst of all, I was afraid of him. Every day I swore I would take no more of his bullying. Yet, every day I considered my cushy life, doing what cats love to do most, nap, sleep, and purr. I knew I should just let it go, turn my tail and skulk back to my cuddly soft bed.

I had not forgotten my frightening struggles on the streets as a stray kitten, but the freedom, which Top Cat enjoyed, purred to me in my dreams. He hunted with an intensity. He prowled through heat, rain, and high winds, like I had done as a kitten. Lean and dirty, he was a persistent predator, because he had to be. He had no home.

He had paraded through the neighborhood like a lion, as if he was king. His swagger and smell imparted fear in many of my friends, it wasn't just me. Top Cat intimidated with his reign of terror, and bullying ways. Danny Cat, who lived a few houses down, and whose only aspiration was to become a Hollywood star, hid under a car every time Top Cat came around.

Then one day, chased by Top Cat, Danny Cat, raced across the street. The timing was bad. Why the cat gods didn't orchestrate the car to hit the bully instead of Danny, I don't know. Seeing Danny's lifeless form crumpled on the asphalt changed me. I snapped. My cushy life, no front claws, my fear, all of that, I buried in the sand. Activate lion mode. I was going to take Top Cat down, dead or alive.

That night was like every other of his nightly visits. Top Cat talked smack to me through the screen, "I'm gonna take everything you have, soft kitty - that rhinestone necklace around your fat neck, your store bought food, and I'll even sleep with your mama." He sneered. I'm gonna grab that scrawny tail of your'n and whip you around 'til you see stars swimming in your head, and then dump you with the fishies in the Pacific."

The comment about sleeping with my Mom is what pushed me to the feral level. I may have been the underdog, with no front claws, and living the good life, but there was only going to be me in Judy's bed.

I had been plotting my revenge for months. I monitored the tabby's wicked, trouble making activities from my various lookouts -the kitchen patio door, the front door, and the bedroom windowsill. Top Cat was a ruthless tracker. He investigated every shrub, rock and tree —all the places of refuge for rabbits, lizards and birds. I ran surveillance on his routine and memorized his ways, I became him. In doing so, Top Cat's life as a drifter drew me in. I envied his tyrannical bearing, his matted, straggly under-cover disguise. His titillating lifestyle instilled a thrill that made me twitter with excitement.

It was a Saturday night, when cats are feeling their catnip. Top Cat arrived later than usual. Judy was in bed. I was relieved she would not be around to become entangled when I doled out my wrath.

He sauntered up to the patio screen door, his white flea collar, like a torch, glowed in the moonlight. He crept with an experienced stealth. I had waited all week to make my move. I hadn't slept. Top Cat was going down, dead or alive. If I survived.

The buzzard cat crashed and rattled against the screen and talked trash about my mom. His words lit my fuse, and I hissed like the flaming end on a dynamite stick. Again, Top Cat stormed the door. I screamed.

ACTIVATE LION MODE

Possessed by a fiery wrath, the inferno in his eyes reflected back at me. I slammed my body against the screen. The metal rattled and banged, the crickets stopped their chorus. He glared, but I sensed his surprise.

Again, the bad cat threw himself at the patio door. His claws embedded and he clung on the wire mesh, his eyes wide. Top Cat's razor nails pierced the screen barrier between us. They glinted like knives in the night. The clamor traveled down the hall, and my ears turned toward the bedroom. Judy did not stir. In bed, she would be safe from my uncontrolled rage, because once released, no one near would be safe.

My formidable opponent had front and back claws. He had fought many battles, I was sure, but I knew things he did not. Growing up with no front claws, I learned to fight with my wits and my teeth.

I threw myself against the door while he still hung on the screen. With his weight and now mine, the door lifted from its tracks and crashed onto the tiled patio, crushing Top Cat beneath it. Perched atop the broken screen door, I waited. Confused, Top Cat no longer focused on taking me down. He squeezed and crawled in a frantic attempt to escape the compressing weight of the door. Reaching the edge, he stood, relieved from the heavy burden.

I pounced. My teeth sank into his neck, and I tasted his blood. His screech like a warrior's cry when death is imminent, echoed into the night

He twisted onto his back, nails extracted, ready to fight to his death. I, too, writhed around in anticipation of his defensive move. The scent of Top Cat's fear triggered my adrenaline, pulsing through my body. My ears lay flat, my eyes narrowed and my tail pointed to the stars. The thrill of impending victory roared from my throat, and my own warrior's call pierced the darkness. Top Cat was going down. No survivors!

My teeth buried in his neck again. I flung him, knowing the force could break his neck. He flew up the air and slammed down on the tile floor. I panted as his still body lay limp, not moving. Every muscle primed, I poised ready to pounce again. His head lifted, he was only dazed. He stood and faced me. I stared him down. His eyes reflected the fury in mine, which glowed with victory. He turned, and then slinked toward the fence. Every muscle in my body twitched, wanting to go another round, finish him off, but I stood my ground. He would not be back. My feline fury had won the battle. I was king. He would carry the message to his wildcat comrades, "Sportster is a true warrior. Let him be."

With the sun peaking over the mountains, I cleaned his stench from my fur, swaggered down the hall, and jumped into bed, finishing the night curled up with my mom.

ACTIVATE LION MODE

CHAPTER THIRTEEN

The park had emptied and an afternoon chill, carried by the lengthening shadows, crept over me. The girl approached the picnic table without noticing me hunched in a clump of grass by the table leg. Her feet shuffled and occasionally dragged along the concrete walk. Her focus on her shoes, she studied the neon orange and pink laces that flogged in the air as she walked. Leaving the path, she came toward me, pulled her cell phone from her pocket and sat down. The laces dangled in front of my nose as she tucked her feet under the bench.

The laces rested, curved and snaky, inches from my face. A flowery scent, like the laundry room at home, emanated from her shoes. I stretched my neck to sniff the bottoms. Her foot began to rock side to side, and the neon strings came alive. My paw shot out and captured their movement.

Was the girl playing with me? I peered up at her. Her head down, she stared at her cellphone, her thumbs dancing on the screen's surface. With my paw, I dragged the bright snakes toward me and grabbed them with my teeth. The girl mumbled something, but continued her texting while I pulled and batted at my prize.

"I can't. I'm grounded." She mumbled as her feet swung out in front of her, ripping my bright colored prey from my teeth. She stomped the ground. "I have to go home," she said aloud to no one as her digits jabbed the screen. Her body tensed and she jerked her feet under her, again. The flying laces slapped my face. I grasped at them again. Maybe she is playing. I chewed on the plastic ends.

Engrossed in our tasks, neither of us noticed the tall girl approach. She sauntered with an air of someone older than the girl with the shoelaces did, but she too lacked any zest. She flopped down on the seat very close to the first girl. "Hey," she said.

The neon laces again yanked from my mouth as the tennis shoes kicked back in front of the texting girl. The younger girl scrunched aside, distancing herself, then glanced over at the intruder. "Hey," she answered back and returned to her texting.

The tall girl pulled a small bag of chips from the pocket of her hoodie. It crackled as she tore it open. She shoved it in my friend's line of vision "You want some?" She said, forcing the texter to look up.

She pulled her attention from her phone, scowled at the stranger and said, "What?"

"What do you mean what? I just thought you might want some." The newcomer dug her fingers into the bag and brought out a few between her fingers, and held them up. Her nails flashed with glitter. "These are like fire. My favorite. My name's Wendy." She shoved the chips in her mouth. The loud crunching hung in the air as she dug in the bag for more.

My new friend with the neon laces, shrugged, tucked her cell into her jean's back pocket, and grabbed a couple, then stared off in the distance.

"I've seen you here before. What's your name?" the lanky girl said. "You live close?"

"Not far." My new friend's cell buzzed repeatedly in her pocket as she stood and faced Wendy. "Look, I gotta go. My folks don't know I'm here." She turned to leave.

"Yeah I know how it is," Wendy said." I got sick of all the rules. Be home by nine. Don't go here, don't go there. Do your homework. Do your chores. I decided I didn't need that shit."

My friend turned back to Wendy, whose bright red lipstick contrasted my friend's, who wore none. Wendy gazed off in the distance, shoveling in more Doritos, and chewing loudly. The young girl studied Wendy then said, "What do you mean? Are you eighteen?"

Wendy didn't turn her head, but looked blankly off into the distance. "I mean I left. I ran away."

"You just left? How did you do that?"

The Wendy's challenging stare met my friend's questioning one. "Nothin to it. I left."

"I'm only twelve. I can't."

The cell phone buzzed repeatedly forcing my friend to pull her gaze away. Checking the screen, she said, "I've gotta go," and turned to leave. As she walked away, over her shoulder she said, "I'm Carolyn. You'll be here tomorrow? I usually come about this time."

Wendy's lips spread in a smile that didn't reach her dull eyes. "Sure. I can do whatever I want."

CHAPTER FOURTEEN

Shortly after my new friend, Carolyn disappeared down the path, Wendy, tossed her Dorito bag on the ground, lit a cigarette and sauntered off. My curious nature piqued, I followed, creeping under the bushes edging the grass.

The passenger door of a black car waiting curbside swung open and Wendy slid into the back seat. The car sped off, half way down the block, before the door slammed shut.

Meandering back to my table, I crawled under it to pass the afternoon. I sniffed at the discarded Dorito bag, but left it. Too spicy for me. Just when I found a comfortable position, the sprinklers popped up, spitting and spraying. I jumped up, hitting my head on the bench seat, and dove for the shelter of the shrubs.

In the bushes shadows I waited for the showers to end. The park, now empty of people, attracted resident squirrels who ventured from their hidey-holes. They scampered around the playground, examining found items and scraps of food from the earlier careless visitors. As I observed the creatures I pondered about how, just like them, there was no one to tell me what to do, which bush I could sniff, or what time I had to go in the house. I did not have to EVER go inside. An urge pulled at me to join the squirrels, but the sprinklers' spray kept me pinned.

I decided the risk of a soaking would be worth the joy of hunting the squirrels. After all living free meant killing for your dinner. A hiss from the spigots ended the raindrops as quickly as they had begun. I flexed my non-existent claws, jerked my tail, and bolted across the wet grass for my closest victim. He saw me approach, so he sat up from burrowing in the dirt, and faced me. Like the ceramic statue at home, he didn't move, but his tail switched and his nose wiggled.

I sprang. Ears back, I shot through the air. My adrenaline pumped and my heart raced. My tail pointed horizontal and straight like an arrow behind me. I would remember this moment forever. My first kill. My prey remained frozen. Was it fear in his eyes? His tail bopped up and down one last time. My mouth salivated, as it anticipated dinner.

He scurried up the nearest tree quicker than a darting hummingbird. In midair, I twisted, my paws grabbed only air. Landing and kicking up dirt, I chased his scent to the tree. Propelled by my back claws, I scaled half way up the trunk, but I lost momentum and leaped back to the ground. My escaped prey danced on the limb above me and chattered with laughter. Flicking my tail, I turned, slashing back and forth in anger as I walked away.

ACTIVATE LION MODE

I hopped up on the bench that the mothers had used and I stretched out. No matter. I caught the last afternoon rays. I inhaled the soft green grass, the water's scent from the spraying spouts, and studied the squirrels as they scurried about ignoring me. Despite my hunting failure, I liked this place. Maybe I would stay. The mothers and their children would be approachable tomorrow. Miss Snow from the shelter had taught me how to schmooze. The women had food stashed in their strollers, and I even smelled milk. My tummy growled at the thought. I glanced at Mellie and Richard's house across the street and considered returning, but the traffic was heavy. I had been lucky crossing the first time. I wasn't going to push my luck with the cat gods

I jumped from the bench seat and padded over to a gang of squirrels arguing over something they had dragged out of a trash receptacle. When I approached, they dropped their prize and scattered. Yes. I was still King. My mouth salivated as I sniffed the left over sandwich. Tuna! My stomach grabbed my gut, yet I took my time and smelled every inch before being assured it was safe to eat. I ate meticulously, small bites, licking up each crumb from the ground. Finishing, I wiped my face and cleaned my paws, then ambled over to a bubbling spigot to wash my dinner down.

The taste of tuna reminded me of Annabelle. I wanted to blame her for my plight. She had brought out the worst in me. If I hadn't tried to play the tough guy, maybe I would still be eating out of a rhinestone dish and sleeping in her plush bed.

I scanned the park. I thought I saw the shadows of Katie and her friend Destiny smiling at me from the swings. I wished I had met Katie when she was a healthy, happy little girl. I looked again, but only empty seats listed in the breeze. The squirrels carped around a picnic table, scolding one another over their loss.

A vision of the motorhome accident sent my heart racing. Flashbacks were becoming a common occurrence. The fear from that day flooded through me. I wanted to cry. If only I had ran over to Judy as she lay on the side of the road. But the iron smell of blood and the frightening growls from the motorhome had kept me frozen, afraid to approach. Where was my courage then? I should have attacked the men before they took her away, at least chased after them. I thought of the kitten I had come upon squashed in the road. Judy had not been dead, but I knew she had been badly hurt. By now, maybe she was dead.

Who was I kidding? How was I going to get home? Instinct told me it was a long, long way. I sighed and returned to the bushes near what I now claimed as my table, and discovered an abandoned burrow. I pushed dried leaves into the tunnel for a mattress. Not like Judy's, but adequate. Curling into a ball, I closed my eyes and hoped the bad dreams would not wake me. I inhaled the musky odor of the outdoors. I'm living in the wild.

****

ACTIVATE LION MODE

Daybreak brought out the birds who chirped as if they attended a homecoming convention. Like the squirrels, they chattered over one another, discussing the day's agenda and the happenings of the night before. A tap, tap, tap reached my ears. I rose, stretched, and peered out from my bush bedroom. Three people, moved from tree to tree, one carrying a stack of papers, another a hammer, and the third directed the crew. "Tack one to the bench over there," she pointed.

The other said, "Some one's bound to have seen him."

By the time woodpecker people left, the papers fluttered on every tree and surface possible. I crept out of my hiding and jumped onto the park bench seat that I now, also, called mine. Laying down, I extended my legs in front and behind me, exposing them to morning's warmth. A flyer nailed to the backrest brushed my ear, tickling it. I shook my head and inspected the paper. The picture portrayed a cat who looked like me it was me! I'd seen enough images of myself in the mirror to recognize my handsome mug.

This was not good. Now, everyone would be looking for me. I've had enough problems on this impossible journey, I did not need any more interference. I checked the scent on the notice. It wasn't Judy's. So, it wasn't her searching for me. My heart twisted. It was time to seriously review my options. My tail twitched, thumping against the seat. I licked my paws, my face and my tail. The habit settled my confusion... and panic.

I decided to go under cover, at least until I could come up with a plan. I dropped down, and slinked back into my burrow. Mothers arrived with strollers and children in tow. Clouds shaded the play area and it began to rain. The women called out to their charges as they yanked jackets from the deep pockets of the carriages, and the gentle downpour washed the air. Only moments passed before they bundled up their darlings and vacated the park.

A raindrop danced on a leaf and swan dived to the one below it, landing with a click. The minute sound combined with the other drops, creating a musical cadence. I shrank deeper into my den when the beads began to beat their rhythm on my head.

As the day passed, I thought of Jawbreaker aka Pit, Tatooman and Guitarman. Wouldn't it be nice if they were here? I ached with loneliness, yet chasing squirrels, and butterflies was like a dream come true. I tightened into a ball and curled my tail over my nose. Sleeping was always a good way to pass the time. When Judy ran errands all day, I worried until she returned. But I could sleep, too, because I had never doubted she would come back through the door.

When the afternoon shadows lengthened, the girls came from opposite directions as if by plan. My new friend, Carolyn, shuffled along with her nose to her cell phone, her thumbs picking at its screen. Her dark, almost black hair hung down like a curtain around her face. The neon laces, which dangled and danced atop her sneakers, were now muddied by the rain. Skinny jeans wrapped tight against ample thighs and pushing a bulging muffin top up and over her waistband that her crop top couldn't hide. Over the shirt, she wore a black hoodie, open in front. She glanced up toward the picnic table where I perched now that the rain had let up.

Our gazes met and I turned my head as if pointing to the approach of Miss Wendy I-do-what I-want.

CHAPTER FIFTEEN

Neither girl spoke, as they plopped across from one another at the picnic table. I sat neatly on the tabletop, my tail curled atop my toes, gazing from one girl to the other. Carolyn with the muddied neon laces held her cell in her right hand and absently reached her left out to me, allowing me to sniff her fingers. She had been eating bacon.

"Is that your cat?" Miss Wendy-do-what-she-wanted stared at me, her eyes glazed with a hardness. One side of her mouth turned downward, pointing to heavy makeup layered over a scar, tracing her jawline.

"No. He was just here." Carolyn scratched my ears again, and I pressed my head against her palm. "I don't think he has a home." Her forehead wrinkled as she turned to Wendy. "What about you? If you left home, where do you live?"

Wendy, engrossed with her own cell said, "Hey chill with all the questions. I have friends. We live across from the high school."

"You just make it sound like you got it made."

ACTIVATE LION MODE

Wendy smirked, ignored the comment, and turned her attention back to her phone.

Carolyn took advantage of the girl's preoccupation and studied her. Her cheekbones protruded, causing her face to appear drawn and triangular. "You got a boyfriend?" Carolyn asked.

Wendy jerked her head up, her downturned mouth twisted into a tight smile that exposed dimples. "Yeah. I got a guy. He takes care of me." She reached out her arm and pointed to a tattoo. "He got me this for my birthday."

My friend leaned in and examined the names inside the red heart -Wendy and then the initial B with a small crown over the letter.

"The B and the crown stands for King Blade. That's what everybody calls him." Her finger caressed the ink." He says this means I belong to him."

"That's nice," Carolyn said and continued to rub my ears as she fiddled with her phone.

"So what's up with you?" Wendy asked. "Why you letting everyone tell you what to do? How old are you, anyway?" She rocked as she swung her legs to and fro.

Carolyn let out a deep breath. "I told you. I'm going to be thirteen in a couple months. My mom and stepdad won't let me do anything." She kicked the table leg and I jumped from the jolt and leaped to the ground. She glanced down at me. "Oh, sorry kitty."

What is it with every one? I'm not some little kitty! I switched my tail, sniffed the grass, and began to follow the scent of a squirrel.

"Oh! I almost forgot." Carolyn dug into the pocket of her hoodie and fished out a small bag. The crackle of plastic and aroma of salmon reached my ears and nose, and I bounded back up on the table. "Wow. You must be hungry," she said.

I pushed my head against the bag, and then pawed at it. "Okay. Okay." She ripped it open, pinched a few morsels, and held them up to me. I sank my teeth on her fingers, and she jerked back.

Oops sorry, but seized the pieces, swallowing them whole. It had been a long time since the tuna sandwich.

Wendy laughed. "What a pig." But she ran her hand gently over my back. I ignored her, focusing on Carolyn for more. This time, more carefully, I nibbled the morsels from her fingertips.

"I'm going to the mall. You want to come?" Wendy tilted her head in the direction of the black Honda parked at the curb. "My friends are waiting for me. They'll give us a lift."

Carolyn's eyes flitted around the park and paused on the car. "I don't know. I should go home." Her brow creased as she wrestled with what to do. "Can they bring me back here by five?" she said. "My folks get home at six. I have to be back before that." I tried to distract her, pushing her hand for more treats. She dumped the contents on the table.

Wendy's face lit up. I sensed her relief, not happiness. "Sure. No prob." She stood, shoved her phone in her back pocket, the flap decorated with rhinestones.

"Are those Miss Me jeans?" Carolyn asked.

"Yeah. You like em? You want to go to Macy's? That's where I got 'em." Wendy slid her hand over her hip, and said, "Nice, huh?"

"Oh my folks would never....."

"Forget them.' Wendy stood up quickly. "Come on, I'll show you how it's done.'" She strode to the car.

Carolyn hesitated only a moment, jumped up and, with a spring to her step, hurried after Wendy, her new I-do-what-I- want-friend while I crunched down the last of the treats,

******

The squirrels scattered at the sound of the car door slamming, and Carolyn's footfall as she ran past them, through the park and approached my picnic table. She threw her shopping bags down next to me, and sank onto the bench, her eyes, once again, fixed on her phone.

"Ugh!" She slammed the phone down on the table. "I hate her." Noticing me at last, I greeted her with a meow and trotted over to her. "Gracie texted me that Tina said I was a bitch 'cause I was talking to her boyfriend. What a grind." She patted my head and I rubbed against her palm. "I hate everyone. My step dad's going to want to know where I got the money for these." She pulled a tank top and jeans from the large bag and held the shirt up against her chest. "What do you think?"

I sniffed it.

"Pretty cool, don't you think?" She peered down at the V-neck, which dove deep, and low. Yeah, I know. I'm screwed. So what's new?" She shoved the purchases back in the bag, checked her watch, and jumped up. "Maybe I'll luck out, and they're running late."

She strode three blocks down the street past Mellie and Richard's, and I padded behind her. Her house nestled in a grove of trees on the rear of a large lot. I followed Carolyn through the empty carport to the back door. "Yes! I beat them home." A beige car turned into the drive as she fiddled with her keys. "Crap," she said, and jerked around. Rushing over to the trashcans against the house, she lifted the lid and shoved her bags inside the grey, recycle one.

ACTIVATE LION MODE

"Hi Honey. You just coming home?" Her mother climbed out of the car, carting a large purse. Her scent reminded me of my visits to the veterinarian, Clorox and alcohol. "Ralph will be along in a minute. He's picking up milk at the store."

Carolyn unlocked the door and held it open for her mom. I slipped in, unnoticed and followed Carolyn as she made her way down the hall to her room. I leaped on the bed.

Her face lit up. "How did you get in here?" She whispered, and quickly shut the door. "You'd better hide. They have a no-pet rule, among all the others." She fell back on the bed, her nose to her phone. I spread out beside her and began cleaning up for dinner.

Carolyn passed the time hiding in her room and texting. Sounds from the kitchen drifted under the bedroom door. Ralph's voice boomed along with the high-pitched words of Carolyn's mother, but Carolyn, with her headphones on, heard nothing.

I jumped when the door opened, and Ralph burst in. "Your mother and I want to see you in the kitchen." A vein in his neck bulged, and his jaw moved as if he were chewing. His focus fell on me. His eyes drew together. "What's that?" His face turned redder. "It seems as if you are bringing all kinds of things home." He spun around, and before he stormed down the hall, he shouted, "In the kitchen. Now."

Carolyn yanked off her earphones and looked at me. "Man, what's their problem, now?" She jumped off the bed, and stomped down the hall. I snuck along behind.

In the kitchen Ralph and her mom sat at the table, her Macy's bag perched between them like a dirty, rotten snitch.

CHAPTER SIXTEEN

Carolyn tensed and stared at the bag. Then her shoulders slumped, but she didn't enter the kitchen. I sat at her feet by the doorway.

Her mother, hands clasped in front of her, with white knuckles, faced Ralph who sat across from her at the dinette. Her stocking feet poked out of the crisp uniform's pants legs, and she had tucked them under the chair. "Sit down," she said.

Carolyn remained fixed at the doorway, but her angry energy begin to boil. She took a deep breath, exhaled hard. I jumped out of the way, as she stomped to the table and plopped into a chair.

"Do you want to tell us about this?" Her mother dumped out the contents of the bag. Ralph sat rigid, his eyes boring into Carolyn's. She glared back at him. His jaw muscles flexed.

Carolyn switched her focus from her step dad and rolled her eyes at her mother. "Wendy and I went to the mall. She bought them for me."

The vein in Ralph's temple bulged, his mouth straight-lined. Carolyn's mother continued the interrogation. "And why was it stuffed in the recycle bin?"

Shoving herself up from the table, the chair scraped across the floor. "Because I knew this is how you would react! I can't do anything without you guys accusing me of something." She grabbed the top and jeans and shoved them into the bag. "This is my stuff, and screw you. I don't have to explain anything." She reached the doorway when Ralph's voice boomed against her back. "Get back in here and sit down." She stopped, squeezed her eyes shut, and grimaced. Twisting around, she glanced down at me. I rubbed against her leg, and let out a small meow, wishing I could help. She hung her head, marched back to the table, and sat down.

The parents exchanged a nod and Ralph asked, "Who is this Wendy? I haven't heard you talk about her. Do we know her?"

"I just met her."

Ralph's eyes shifted to his wife then back to Carolyn. "You just met her, and she bought you over a two hundred dollars' worth of clothes?" He shook his head. His features sagged. "Carolyn, no one just buys you stuff, especially a stranger. She had to have some angle."

"There you go! Big time badass Sergeant Meeker! Always judging people. Can't someone just be nice? Not everyone is bad. Just 'cause you're a cop, you think everyone is out to get me."

"Look, Carolyn, maybe your friend's just being nice, but until we meet her, I don't want you going places with her. And because you broke the rules by not coming straight home from school, your mother and I are putting you on restriction for a week. After that, why don't you invite Wendy over to the house?"

"Man! What am I supposed to do every afternoon for three or four hours? You guys never get home 'til six or even later."

Pain twisted Carolyn's mother's face, and her hand wiped across her mouth as if trying to erase the expression. She reached for her daughter's hand. "I will try to get home earlier."

"Yeah sure." Carolyn jerked her hand away and picked at the polish on her fingernails then glared at Ralph. "Are we done here?"

Ralph and Mom traded worried expressions. Ralph's forehead creased with deep lines as he motioned to me. "Open up a can of tuna for that cat. Did you find him in the park, too?"

"I don't think he has a home." Carolyn's face softened. "Can I keep him?"

Ralph sighed. "We'll see."

Carolyn removed a can of tuna from the cupboard and opened it. As fast as she spooned the fishy chunks into a ceramic dish, I scarfed them up and then washed it all down with water from the matching bowl beside it.

"Are you using my good dishes?" Mom peered down at me. "We should check the pound to see if someone's looking for him. I wonder if he's been chipped."

Her daughter squatted down and ran her hand over my back. "Why can't we keep him?"

Mom rose from the table, and knelt down by her daughter. I rushed her, pressing my head into her extended palm. "I don't know, honey. It's up to Ralph. Anyway he might belong to someone."

Carolyn shot back up, threw the spoon into the sink, and stormed down the hall. "It's always what Ralph wants! No one cares what I want!" Her bedroom door slammed.

Mom rose and collapsed into the chair next to Ralph, who took her hand and squeezed it. "She needs to cool off. We'll talk to her tomorrow." He slumped, shaking his head. "I just remembered. I'm not sure of my schedule the next few days. We're in the middle of planning a sting operation."

She shuddered and he wrapped an arm around her shoulders. "Don't worry. You've raised her well.

She's just going through a rebellious stage. She'll do the right thing if it comes down to the wire."

Mom hung her head and tears dropped softly on the table. "All I can think of is Lois and JR. and what they're going through. I always thought they raised Kylie right, but she's been missing for a month now, without a trace. Poor Lois, I don't know how she's holding up. I call her every day. I was going to have Carolyn go with me this weekend to help distribute flyers."

Ralph rubbed her back. "I think Carolyn should get involved. I know she didn't know Kylie, but Carolyn needs to be aware of what's going on. It would be an education for her."

"Oh Ralph, If you saw some of the girls they bring into emergency, especially those strung out on drugs. One was in labor. She was only twelve years old!" She buried her face in Ralph's chest.

"You forget what I see on the streets," Ralph said, as he continued to massage her back. "When they get a girl, they do what they call 'seasoning.' It's a trust-building period like they do in cults, and they can be extremely patient, wining and dining a girl, giving her whatever she wants. They are masters at singling out a vulnerable girl at a mall or high school campus. The girls in the life call it 'spitting the game.' During that honeymoon stage they ask the girl if she has any friends who are discontented like she is and she'll unknowingly end up bringing her friends in."

Mom took a deep breath and pulled away from him. She looked into his eyes. "I'm going to take a leave of absence. It's the only way." She stood up. "I know money'll be tight, but I have to do this." She wrung her hands and began to pace. Her voice carried an excited hopefulness. "I've got to reconnect with Carolyn. It's the only way."

Ralph pushed himself from the table as if still bound in his Kevlar vest and carrying the weight of all his gear. Pulling his wife close, he kissed her. "Whatever you decide, honey. We'll make it. Right now, I've got paperwork to do. Call me when dinner's ready? I'll check out the noise in the washer too."

After Ralph left, I rushed Mom and began weaving around her legs. She smiled at down atme and said, "Why don't you go see Carolyn? She could use a friend." I trotted in front of her as she led me down the hall, Mom came up behind. "Maybe you can talk to her," she said, opening Carolyn's door a crack. I rushed in as she closed it quietly behind me.

CHAPTER SEVENTEEN

Carolyn slammed her backpack on her bed so hard it bounced as I slipped into the room. She spun around to her dresser, yanked open a drawer and grabbed an armful of clothes. Catching sight of me, she said. "I don't have to take this shit. They don't want to hear about how the girls called me crashy at school today, and how even my GF's laughed. I'm not going back to school. Wendy told me to text her anytime and she'd come pick me up."

I trotted over to a scrunchie that bounced to the floor and I attacked it. Grasping it in my paws, I rolled over and kicked it until the fabric-covered elastic flew in the air. I sprang up, pounced again, and repeated my antics.

"Hey! That's for my hair." She knelt down and tugged at the accessory, but I clamped my teeth and pulled back... "Let go." She giggled, and I relaxed my hold. "Hey, you can go with me." I jumped onto the bed and stretched out across her backpack. I knew all about packing, but this time no one was packing for me.

Carolyn and I passed the evening tossing the scrunchie back and forth in between her texting. Sounds from the kitchen quieted and changed to soft noises from the TV in the den. I scratched at the bedroom door.

"Do you need to go potty?"

Carolyn opened her door, and I rushed down the hall. Going to the bathroom outside was an inconvenience of my new lifestyle with which I was learning to deal. Memories of Judy and my private bathroom in our motorhome filled my mind. Carolyn followed me to the back door and let me out. "I'll come out after they go to bed."

I stepped into the cool air and exhaled a tiny whimper. I missed Judy and my quiet easy routine with her. My thoughts drifted to the night of the accident and I trembled as I relived the scene. My sense of direction told me I wasn't very far from the crash site, and still a long way from home. I wandered over to the rose bushes alongside the garage and sniffed around. I regretted my wish from a lifetime ago, of wanting to live in the wild. I didn't have a litter box. - My favorite catnip toy that soothed me when I licked the scented bundle was lost - Judy's lap, along with her hugs and kisses that I hated - I missed them all. I ached for familiarity, the comfortable scents of home and Judy.

I found a spot, did my business and covered it. I started to return to the house, but had to stop and clean my paws, now soaked in mud. A moth flitted past, but I ignored the opportunity to take chase. Instead, I padded toward the back door, and crouched on the cold concrete steps.

ACTIVATE LION MODE

A drizzle began, softly dripping from the eaves. I wanted the warm, dry motorhome's dashboard where I perched and watched the rain. I wanted to drink from the faucet instead of a muddy puddle. I curled up in a ball of depression and sadness, closed my eyes, and dozed.

I smelled him before I heard him rattle the trash can. He stood on his hind legs, his claws stretched to the lid, which had not been tightly secured. In the moment it took to flick my tail in alarm, he had brought the container crashing to the ground, the contents spilling out onto the patio. He rooted through the assorted bags of garbage ripping them open, his erect tail pointed skyward, a glowing white stripe tracked down his tail, the length of his body, to the tip of his nose. Feasting on an apple core, he paused and looked challenging in my direction. Suddenly the porch light flooded the area and he scurried away just as the back door's lock clicked and the door swung open.

Ralph stepped outside taking in the garbage strewn everywhere "What's going on?" He looked at me huddled on the step. "What have you done? So you're a dumpster diver, are you?" He made his way over to the scene of the crime, assuming I was the guilty culprit. He up-righted the bin, and began picking up the trash. "Didn't you get enough to eat? Well, if you're still here tomorrow, we'll get you some real cat food. Okay, Buddy?" I followed him around, rubbing his leg as he picked up the last of the mess, thankful he wasn't angry even though he blamed me. He shoved the final bundle into the can and headed back in the house. Holding open the door, he pointed inside and said, "Come on, Buddy. Don't you want to come in out of the rain?"

I stared at him, but didn't accept his invitation.

"Okay, buddy. I guess you have your reasons."

***

"Where are you?" She whispered as she shuffled down the steps wrestling with her bulging backpack and a garbage bag full of clothes. I ran to her from my dry hiding spot by the garage, chirping as I went. "I'm glad you waited. Come on let's get out of here." She hiked down the drive, hefting the bag over her shoulder while the backpack bounced against her. I trotted ahead, recognizing the black car that had been at the park. It idled at the curb, its lights off.

As she and I approached, the rear passenger door it opened and Wendy gestured with a wave. "Get in, "she said.

I slipped in behind Carolyn, squeezing past her feet. Wendy and another girl, whose heavy scent reminded me of the flowers by the garage, sat in the back seat. Another girl sat in the front and smelled more like smoke. It must have been Wendy's boyfriend driving. A baseball cap, its bill turned backwards, donned his baldhead, and tattoos covered his thick, bare arms. No one but Wendy paid us any mind. "You're lucky," she said. "We're on our way to a party."

ACTIVATE LION MODE

Conversation was limited. Carolyn's nervousness filled the car's interior. The girl beside Carolyn kept her head down, but her dark eyes rolled up, first to the couple in the front seat, and then back to her fingernails as she picked and nibbled on them. Wendy stared out into the passing darkness. The girl beside the driver snuggled and kissed him. Maybe he wasn't Wendy's boyfriend.

The boyfriend, or whoever he was, turned the car into an inlaid brick drive and pulled up to a wrought iron gate with a guardhouse. The headlights lit up the guard who trod toward the vehicle, palm resting on his holstered weapon. The so-called boyfriend rolled down his window and said, "Just delivering the entertainment." The guard stuck his head inside, eyeing the girls.

He nodded. "Save a piece of the cake for me," he said, and pressed a button on his belt.

The boyfriend chuckled and reached out the open window for a high five. "You got it, Bro." The gate creaked and crawled open. He stepped on the gas and the tires screeched as the vehicle lurched through the gate.

~~JUDY HOWARD~~ SPORTSTER THE CAT

CHAPTER EIGHTEEN

I leapt onto Carolyn's lap as the car sped down the tree-lined entrance. Approaching the circular drive, the vehicle's black hood reflected the solar lights strung along the walkway. The boyfriend pulled behind several limos whose tuxedoed drivers stood guard like stable boys at the racetrack. A motorhome at the far curve of the drive rumbled and growled. Its dark tinted windows and sweeping gold and black body paint vibrated from the idling diesel engine.

A dark mood settled inside the Honda's interior and the girls sank deeper into their seats. The boyfriend killed the engine, exited the vehicle. He strutted around the vehicle and yanked open the back passenger door. His fingers curled over the edge of the door, holding it open. Carolyn peered up. Her heart pounded. He reached out his hand, encrusted with gold rings, and Carolyn took it. His grasp was gentle, and his smooth-shaven face spread in a large smile. Carolyn relaxed as she stepped out of the car. Ignoring the other girls, he steered Carolyn toward the palatial front door. I followed them up the walk.

Muted music pulsed from inside. A sweet smelling smoke, tangled with a sharp chemical odor greeted us. Wendy shot Carolyn a hard look as she and the other two girls pushed past her and the boyfriend. I didn't want to lose track of Carolyn so I grabbed my last deep breath of cool evening air and slipped in behind them.

ACTIVATE LION MODE

The room could house three motorhomes like the one in the driveway. Two large screen TVs displayed talking heads, which droned on with predictions of the latest sports scores, spreads, and court cases of the games and their players. The party goers sparkled with super bowl rings and gold studs, and flashed confident attitudes that the girls in the Honda did not.

Carolyn and the boyfriend paused in the doorway. "Come on I'll stay with you, show you around," he said. He moved in beside her, his hip against hers, his cold, gold rings slid across her bare mid drift. He leaned down close to her ear. "You're lookin' good. The guys are gonna flip when they meet you. But don't worry I'll keep an eye on them." The boyfriend introduced her around the room chatting easily with the guests.

I took my position under a chair that afforded a view of the room.

After making the rounds, the boyfriend led Carolyn back near my chair. Carolyn sipped from a pink drink and then gazed down at a small box he held in his palm. He flipped it open, pulling out a glittering gold necklace, and dangled it from his long fingers. She reached over and touched the sparkling jewel.

"Wendy told me all about you, but I never expected you to be so beautiful. The moment I saw you, I wanted you." When he tilted his head, his eyes appeared to glow red like the stone.

Carolyn's eyes flashed back and forth from him to the jewel and back again.

"I know it sounds crazy." He swept down, kissed her, nibbling her lip, and then quickly stepped back. Shaking his head, he said, "I'm sorry, I couldn't resist. You probably have a boyfriend."

Carolyn touched her lips where his had brushed hers, her face red as the gem she now held in her hand.

"Here," he said, "Let me see what it looks like on." Standing behind her, he draped the necklace around her neck.

Carolyn eyes caught sight of Wendy. Her friend's arms wrapped around the neck of a distinguished, thick-waisted man with salt and pepper hair wearing a Polo shirt and brown slacks. His gravelly voice carried across the room. It rose and fell with an increased energy as he responded to Wendy who pressed up against him.

The boyfriend turned Carolyn around to face him. His thin fingers traced around the jewel nestling on her breastbone, then tracked up the length of the gold chain, disappearing behind the hair on her neck. He pulled her to him and kissed her again, this time hard on the lips. Still she stood motionless and confused, but her heart pounded.

He pulled away. "I've got to take you home."

Carolyn eyes grew big. "But why? I don't want to go home."

I thought she might cry.

"Did I do something wrong?"

His smile didn't reach his eyes and a dark energy charged through him. He touched her chin. "Oh, no, beautiful one. The only thing you're guilty of is driving me completely crazy. You are too good for me. You should go home."

Her hand clasped the necklace. "No!" She was crying now. "I don't want to go home. I hate it there! They won't let me do anything."

His fingers crept up behind her neck, and I thought he would kiss her again. I jumped up on the coffee table and pawed for her attention. She gave me a quick glance.

"Are you sure? Because you could come stay with me." His hand clung to the back of her neck. "But you would have to do what I say."

I pushed hard against her leg. I wanted her to know I was there for her, that she should stick with me, she didn't need this guy.

"I'll do whatever. I won't be any trouble. Just don't send me home."

His smile kinked at the corner. "I think I love you, Baby. How could you be any trouble?"

He looked down at me with his hard eyes. "Is that your cat?"

She quickly scooped me up. "He's kind of adopted me." She rubbed my ears and rolled her eyes up at the man. "Can he come, too?" He paused to answer, frowning as if his decision was a weighty one. "Are you kidding? I would do anything for you."

Crying, Carolyn threw her arms around the boyfriend. "Oh thank you! I won't be any trouble. I promise." She stepped back, wiping her eyes. "I don't even know your name."

"Just call me Blade."

CHAPTER NINETEEN

Carolyn grasped me so tightly I squirmed and jumped down onto the coffee table. Blade steered her to the glittering glass bar, crowded with partygoers. Every female showed a lot of mid drift and leg. The men's ages varied, but each had the attention of at least two girls, or more. Wendy exited the room with her silver haired gentleman followed by the two girls that had ridden in the car. As Blade offered Carolyn another pink drink, I licked some white powder off my paws.

Within moments, a floating sensation overwhelmed me and my tongue became numb. Unsteady, I laid down on the glass table. My stomach churned while my head spun. I hurled. The tuna from dinner spewed onto the tabletop. I looked around. No one noticed. I felt better immediately, staggered off the table, and crawled under it.

When my head cleared, I was certain the suspicions I'd harbored about this place and these people were justified. This was a bad situation. I wanted to leave, but I didn't want to leave Carolyn.

The crowded room thinned out while the loud, harsh musical night wore on. Couples and trios disappeared down the hallway. Wendy and Blade remained in the big room on the sofa. His controlled smile had captured her and she laughed. Uninhibited, she flung her body against him and he feigned surrender, falling back on the couch. Carolyn threw herself on top of him, kissing him, her innocence drowned by the contents of her drink.

Still jittery, I left my safe position and plodded over to the couch. I leaped up onto the sofa's back, missed my mark, and fell to the floor. I arched my back and hissed to cover my embarrassment. On the second try, I succeeded. Carolyn possessed an abandon, which frightened me. She paid me no mind. Steeling myself, because I didn't want to touch Blade, I jumped down, and wedged my way between the two of them.

"Oh, Cat." Carolyn pulled away from her entanglement.

My ploy worked. Blade's mouth twisted and his eyes fixed on me. His intensity frightened me, but I turned my butt to his face and poured my affections on Carolyn. Finally, her state of passion focused on my distraction, and she began to hug and kiss me.

Blade, in his expertise at 'spitting the game,' showed steeled control. His practiced smile returned, and he reached to run his hand over me, pretending to pet me. I spun around, hissed, and spit my own game. The dissension went unnoticed by Carolyn, who floated with the effects of the drinks and whatever else she had consumed. Blade, on the other hand, glared and I knew it was only Carolyn's presence and his patience with her 'seasoning' that saved my life.

I continued to distract Carolyn, rescuing her innocence as she delighted in my lavish purring attention.

"Let's get out of here." Blade pushed me and Carolyn aside, and rose up off the couch. He took Carolyn's arm, pulled her up, and I leaped to the floor. "Pretty young girls like you need your sleep. Come on, I'll show you my place." Carolyn swayed as she stood, and I was careful to avoid her feet as she stumbled to catch her balance.

Wendy reentered the room and Blade motioned to her. Nodding in response his unspoken command, she proceeded to the bar and leaned up close to an athletic young man who sat alone. She smiled and began rubbing her hip against his.

When Blade escorted Carolyn outside, a valet signaled to a chauffeur waiting by a limo. Their ride pulled up to the curb.

The attendant opened the door, and Blade's long finger pressed against Carolyn's bare mid-drift, nudging her into the car. She began to get in, then paused. "Where's Cat?" She said. "You said he can come."

"You don't need a cat." Blade pushed her toward the limo's interior.

Carolyn's mood whipped around, flashing distress. "He's homeless! He needs me. We can't leave him here." The whites of her eyes blazed hot with anger. "You promised!"

Blade's eyes morphed into slits that glowed white like coals in the darkness. He smiled but his jaw muscles flexed as he grit his teeth.

On cue, I appeared and pranced toward Carolyn. I passed by Blade, paused, and then hissed a him. My hair stood on end and my back arched

"There you are, Cat."

I jumped in the limo.

Carolyn climbed in after me. Blade, though rigid with rage, smiled, and then joined us.

His eyes slashed across my body and the heat of his hatred should have singed my fur. I controlled my urge to sink my fangs into the soft flesh of his arm when he reached up to touch Carolyn's face. I, too, could do a little seasoning. I gritted my teeth and rubbed against his offending limb. At first, he jerked at my touch, but then allowed my false affections. Under my fur, my own jaw muscles tightened in restraint.

"See? He's a sweet cat." Carolyn massaged my back instead of Blade's. The valet shut the door, and Carolyn's new family sped off down the drive.

CHAPTER TWENTY

The limo crept down the long drive and approached the gate, which began to slide open. Blade waved, his teeth flashed from his big grin, as the limo glided past the guards.

And then, all hell broke loose.

Black shapes armed with automatic weapons sprang from the thick shadow of trees lining the drive.

"Freeze!! Drop the weapons!!" The threatening shouts erupted from everywhere. Four police cars jerked to a halt in front of the limo. The doors flung open, exposing more menacing shotguns like the claws on a tiger. The guards froze then dropped their shotguns and surrendered.

Blade's long fingers lifted his pant leg. Reaching inside his boot, he dug out a pistol strapped to his ankle. The energy inside the car spit with the electricity of a terrorized wildcat, pulling Carolyn out of her stupor. She stared at the gun in Blade's hand. Her eyes widened as her mind perceived the situation. She grabbed me hard, clutching me so tightly I could hardly breathe.

"Every one out of the car!"

Time seemed to freeze. Nothing moved except Blade's long finger as it curled around the gun's trigger. His anger swelled like the cornered animal he was. He spat at the driver. "Don't move," then glowered at Carolyn. "That means you, too."

"You don't have a chance," said a voice I recognized.

"What do you want me to do, Boss?" The driver said.

"You're going to drive out of here," Blade said. "I've got the get-out-of-jail-free-card sitting right here next to me." His eyes burned into Carolyn's who had not moved, but her heart raced. "It's time to do what I say, pretty one." He pulled her to him, pressed her cheek to his and rolled down the window. He leveled gun barrel against her temple.

Carolyn cried openly. Her entire body trembled, but she didn't let go of me.

"Hey, you pricks." Blade yelled out. "You might want to rethink your position here? Before this pretty little girl gets hurt?"

Blade held her face to the open window. Carolyn gasped as she looked out, locked eyes with the lead officer standing in the forefront, and cried out, "Ralph!" She struggled to free herself, loosening her hold on me.

Blade jammed the muzzle hard against her. "You're the daughter of a dirty rotten cop?"

ACTIVATE LION MODE

She slumped back against the seat. "He's my stepdad."

"Well, how sweet is that?" He yanked her back to the window. "What's his name?"

"Sergeant Ralph Meeker."

"You hear that, Meeker? I got your pretty little daughter here. You don't want anything happening to her, do you?"

Carolyn's frightened sobs shook her body. I peered out the window and Ralph tortured eyes met mine.

"That's what I thought. Tell your men to back off." Blade's fear diminished and his confidence flared up from what I knew was a false sense of security. We were not getting out of here that easy. Ralph was not a man to mess with. The unobtrusive demeanor and deceiving calmness masked a ferocity, which under threatening circumstances, was deadly. Ralph would save the day, but he might need a little help.

CHAPTER TWENTY-ONE

Blade twisted in his seat, uncomfortable with Ralph's lack of response. He may be patient in seasoning a girl to bring to his stable, but his short-lived confidence was dying fast. The smell of his adrenaline hung in the closeness of the car and his evil heart pounded against his chest. Sweat beads joined in rivulets, which snaked down and eroded the steely-smoothness of his face.

Ralph still held my gaze. He slowly closed his eyes and then opened them. He was probably saying a prayer, but I read the slow blink as a sign of trust. Did he know that? My imagination went wild. Was he signaling me to trust him? Or was he saying that he trusted me to save the day? Ralph turned to his men who huddled around him. Their heads bobbed as he barked out instructions I could not hear.

Blade inhaled deeply. "Hey, Ralph. Tell your copper friends I ain't got all day. Me and Carolyn here can't wait to get home and get down and dirty. I've got a lot of moves to teach this young sweet thing. She's never gonna want to come home when I get done with her."

Ralph swung around and faced us. He and I locked eyes again. I thought he nodded to me. I interpreted his signal, took a deep breath, and held it.

ACTIVATE LION MODE

Gritting my teeth, I jumped up on Blade's shoulder. My movement startled the creep, but he held his grip on the Magnum as I rubbed against his ear. I felt the gold studs dig into my cheek as I stretched around and pressed against his nose. My body blocked his view so he twisted away, but I was already climbing onto his bald head.

Blade swung his head to the side. "Get out of here!" He reached up to push me away, releasing his hold on Carolyn who immediately scooted across the seat and grabbed for the door handle. With his view obstructed, Blade focused on shoving me away. I dug my back nails into his pretty face for support as my front legs wrapped around his shaved, tatted head. "You stupid cat!" He turned the gun and aimed at me.

Outside, Ralph stood by his sharpshooter who already had a bead on Blade… and me. A steady red laser lit up the red ink eyes of the blue serpent tatted along Blade's jugular. This was not the laser dot I chased at home with Judy. I pinned my ears back and sank my teeth into the tight neck muscle that made the snake tattoo squirm. Blade screeched only a second before the heat of the sharpshooter's bullet rushed past my ear and penetrated his forehead.

I lunged out the open window as his head pitched back, lolled to the side and then came to a rest and dangled out the window. Seeking safety under the limo, I peeked up. King Blade's vacant eyes, not much different than before, stared down at me.

Carolyn's screams joined the swat team's shouts to the driver. "Come out with your hands up."

As the driver exited, the click, released the door locks, freeing Carolyn from her cage of terror. She burst out, almost falling, and ran to Ralph.

Ralph lowered his weapon and thrust it toward an officer beside him. He opened his arms as Carolyn flung herself into his embrace. They both fell to their knees, and he rocked her as she sobbed. Eager to offer my own soothing purrs, I ran to them.

Carolyn squealed in relief as I wormed my way in between her and Ralph. "Oh Cat! You were so brave!" Ralph held her in a snug embrace while she wrapped me tight in her arms. "You could have been killed!" We rubbed against each other's noses, and she covered my face with kisses.

My murmured meows went unheard because harsh, heated voices sounded everywhere. The metallic clicking of cuffs, rifles, and ammo magazines encircled us while Ralph soothed his stepdaughter. "It's okay, baby. Everything's all right now. You're safe." I guessed he said the words just as much for his own benefit as for Carolyn's. I purred, pushing intensely against her cheek. When Ralph finally stood, he helped his stepdaughter to her feet while she still clutched me. He motioned to a female officer standing by. "Take her home, Marcy." The woman, whose gear on her belt and vest weighed more than she did escorted Carolyn and me to an empty squad car.

ACTIVATE LION MODE

More vehicles entered the crime scene and joined the unit as they all sped up the long drive to surround the mansion full of partygoers.

Marcy eyed us in the rearview mirror. "That's some cat you have there," Marcy said. She steered the vehicle away from the scene, one I was certain Carolyn would never forget. I knew I wouldn't.

Images of my Judy and of the wreckage I had left behind in the Olympic Forest appeared fresh in my mind as if they had occurred yesterday. Suddenly, like an old rotted tree, my body was heavy and weak with sorrow. An ache crept through my bones from my nose to my tail. In this strange aftermath, loneliness consumed me, sweeping over me like the shadow of large bird of prey. I revisited the accident in my mind. I had done nothing to rescue Judy and I had been wracked with guilt since. I chirped a tiny meow, and Carolyn looked down at me. "Don't worry, cat. You're okay now." She placed a long kiss on top of my head. "I love you, Cat."

But I could not stop thinking of Judy. Memories of her erupted. How foolish of me to believe I would ever see her again. How long had it had been already since I'd seen her? I've lived in the wild, fished and hunted. I made friends. More stabs of sadness cut through me as I recalled Jawbreaker, Tattooman and Guitarman. The image of Miss Snow White emerged. Without her guidance, I would not have survived. And Katie. Had I made a difference in her short little life? Now, Carolyn regarded me as her savior. But I am a

~~JUDY HOWARD~~ SPORTSTER THE CAT

traitor. I mewed for Judy. Exhaustion seeped into my bones. I curled in Carolyn's lap and closed my eyes.

ACTIVATE LION MODE

CHAPTER TWENTY-TWO

Daybreak was dissolving the black night as Marcy opened the police cruiser door. Rousing me awake, Carolyn climbed out, just as her mother burst from the carport and rushed to her daughter. On impact, she grasped us and squeezed hard.

She leaned back to look her daughter. "Are you okay, baby?" Her teary eyes darted from Carolyn up to the officer.

Marcy smiled and nodded. "She's fine. Just a little shook up."

"Ralph told me what happened." Again, she clutched us, then leaned back once more, and glared at her daughter. Her hands grabbed Carolyn's shoulders and she shook us. "What were you thinking?"

. I squirmed to get away. This might turn ugly, but Carolyn only cried. Her mascara outlined her red eyes. The girl peered up at her mother like a small kitten. "I'm so sorry, Mom. I was so scared!" Still clenching me, Carolyn flung herself against her mother and sobbed.

I squirmed again. The situation diffused. I needed air.

Carolyn pulled away from her mother and began kissing me on the head again. "Oh, Mom. You should have seen how brave Cat was. He attacked that jerk so I could get away."

Her wet face rubbed against mine.

"He was so brave! He could have been killed!"

I rubbed my cheek against hers.

With big eyes, Carolyn looked up at her mom. "Ask Ralph. Cat saved me. He's a hero."

"You can tell us all about it, Honey. Come on in the house, you too, Cat. I'll bet you're both hungry." Mom glanced up at Marcy, whispered a thank you, and herded us into the house. Mom hustled us to the kitchen table where less than twenty-four hours ago an innocent, defiant young girl, afraid of nothing, had wanted to take on the world Mom caressed her daughter's back. "If Cat is such a hero, you're going to have to think of a heroic name for him."

"You mean we can keep him?" Carolyn's eyes grew big, her brow raised. Hope flittered across her face.

Mom reached over and scratched my head. "I have no doubt. Now, would you like some breakfast?"

I jumped down and checked my dish. Empty. I studied Carolyn and her mother who now stroked her daughter's hair. My new family. Like Carolyn, the desire to be on my own had driven me to be in the wild and

ACTIVATE LION MODE

conquer the world, but life was full of Top Cats and tough guys like Blade. I bellowed out a long meow.

Sure, I had overcome the obstacles. I had achieved my dream and gained a confidence I would never lose. I sat beside my dish while Mom talked to Carolyn and showered her daughter with motherly affections. This was a nice enough family. I knew I had won over Ralph. I could live here. I had to accept I was never going to see Judy again. My life lessons taught me to face reality. I sighed and sniffed the empty dish again. I wasn't hungry anyway. Turning, I padded down the hall, jumped up on Carolyn's bed and curled into a tight ball. I was cold, and very, very tired.

CHAPTER TWENTY-THREE

I opened my eyes halfway when Carolyn entered the room and flopped onto the bed. She rolled over, facing me, and fingered my collar. "Oh, Cat. I love you so much. First thing I'm going to do is buy you a new collar with lots of jewels. And you need a name tag, too. She curled her arm around me and quickly fell asleep.

The entire day had passed. The room had turned to dark greys when a light tap on the door awakened us, and Ralph entered. His eyes had softened from the last time I'd seen him at the take down at the mansion, but his lips remained stretched in a tight line across his twelve-hour beard. His hair clung, mashed and sweaty, flat against his head. "Dinner's ready, Munchkin. Wash up." He paused a moment, waiting until she moved. She stretched slowly first then suddenly popped up, eyes wide, straight backed, holding her breath. Then her back curved in relaxation and she exhaled.

"It's okay Munchkin. You're home now." Her eyes met his, and she scrambled out of bed, running to him.

He stood stiffly while Carolyn grasped him in a desperate hug. "Oh Ralph, I'm so sorry. I'm so sorry." She buried her face in his chest as his strong arms wrapped around her.

ACTIVATE LION MODE

His thick-fingered hand patted her back. "It's okay now. You're safe. Everything's all right, now."

"But I was so scared ... I thought Blade was ... OMG. I'm so stupid." She cried. He grabbed her shoulders, gently pushing her away, and turned her chin up, forcing her teary eyes to focus on his intense, steady ones. "Look Carolyn, you aren't stupid. You're only young and innocent. That's why your mother and I worry so much."

"Yes but..." He laid his fingers across her lips.

"We'll talk more later. Let's go to dinner." His tight lips melted into a warm smile, and his eyes watered as he cleared his throat.

Carolyn nodded, wiped her nose with her arm, and turned to me. "Come on Cat." Ralph nestled his stepdaughter under his arm and guided her down the hall.

I proceeded directly to my dish. My dinner waited. The aroma wafted up, smelling like the little fish I'd caught in the river at the Olympic forest. My tummy twisted, and I squeezed out a tiny whimper as I envisioned that little guy swimming frantically back to his school. I turned away and hunched down by the doorway

Mom set the casserole in the middle of the table. "It's your favorite, Baby, Chili Mac, but eat your salad first." Mom took her place, and the room warmed with low talk – 'pass the rolls and the dressing, please.' 'Thank yous', and 'it's really good' joined the clinks of silver against glass, plates, and bowls.

Ralph hovered over his plate, devouring his serving of chili mac. Chewing a mouthful, he peered up at Carolyn. "I met your friend Wendy."

"Omg! I almost forgot about her. Is she okay?" Carolyn's wide eyes met Ralph's.

Ralph held Carolyn's expectant gaze for a moment. "We took her to juvie. Booked her on prostitution."

Carolyn's mouth dropped open. She dropped her fork. "Prostitution? She was just like me! How could you? She was just there to party. She thought Blade was her boyfriend, too. How could you?"

Ralph turned to Mom in a silent request for help. Mom said, "Look Carolyn, these were some bad and dangerous people you were mixed up with. Wendy was not just a partygoer. She was Blade's number one girl in his prostitution ring. She was not your friend."

Carolyn started to say something, but instead picked up her fork and poked at her salad. "I don't understand."

Mom reached over and covered Carolyn's hand with her own. "Honey, we've tried to tell but you didn't want to listen. Maybe we should have done more."

Carolyn curled her fingers around her mother's hand and squeezed. The young girl's expression reflected more than sadness. "No mom. You're right. You and Ralph tried to tell me. I should have listened." Carolyn straightened as if determined to shake off her naiveté. With pretended coolness, she focused on Ralph. "I'm ready to listen."

CHAPTER TWENTY-FOUR

Ralph cleaned his plate with the last bite of his dinner roll and hungrily shoved the morsel in his mouth. His whiskered cheeks puffed out as he chewed and I thought of Jaw Breaker, the veterans' pit-bull from the Olympic forest. Jawbreaker's cheeks puffed out when he ate, too. The dog's big heart loved Tattooman, Guitarman and even me. I recalled the comfort in knowing the dog would risk his life for any of us.

Ralph shoved his dish to the side, inhaled deeply, and glanced at Mom. She nodded. His serious eyes tracked back to his stepdaughter. He studied her questioning face while his own displayed a jadedness for the task before him. His shoulders slumped, as if the responsibility of explaining life to his twelve-year-old stepdaughter was too much

"Blade's a pimp, not a boyfriend. Do you know what a pimp is?" Ralph watched Carolyn's features as if he were interrogating her.

"Sure. A pimp's a black guy who has a bunch of women working for him who hang out on street corners, and take men to crummy hotels."

"That's the general impression, but pimps can be anybody, any race. When a girl first meet a pimp, he's very charming. He buys her things, and treats her like a princess, like Blade did. That's how pimps reel girls in. Didn't you think Blade cared about you? Maybe you thought you loved him?"

Carolyn hung her head. "I was so stupid."

"No Carolyn. You were just being the sweet inexperienced girl that you are. Pimps prey on girls like you who are tired of all the rules at home. The ones who just want to have a boyfriend. He's a professional at what they call 'seasoning'. Even if we hadn't come along and exposed him for the criminal he is, you would have eventually been faced with his violent side, but by then, it would have been too late. He would already have shipped you off far from here, and you would never have been able to come home."

Carolyn shook her head. "It' so hard to believe what you're saying. If I could forget the gun and how scared I was… and what almost happened to poor Cat…." She swung around, rose and swooped me up in her arms. Cradling me, she sat back down, and her doe eyes stared at Ralph. "I want to blame it all on you. If you hadn't showed up, he wouldn't have acted like that. You made him act like that. He couldn't help it."

Ralph dropped his gaze to the tabletop. "Carolyn …"

"No. I know it's true, what you're saying. I'll never forget what happened. Never." Her eyes welled with tears that overflowed and drained into my fur. "Oh God. How will I ever forget?" She buried her face against me.

Mom reached over, and patted her daughter's shoulder. "You're safe now, Baby."

Carolyn raised her head. "I liked Wendy. So you think she was one of his girls like you say?" She looked at Ralph, her pleading expression tugged at my heart as it did Ralph's. Mom sat quietly, her own sorrow pooling on the tabletop.

"She was."

"Do you think she wants to go home?"

"I'm sure she did once, but she might have given up the hope."

Carolyn stared at nothing as her mind processed the ugly information of the past eight hours. Dark circles under her bloodshot eyes blended into smeared mascara and accented her ashen face. "I'm tired. I want to go to bed."

She rose and Mom jumped up, hugging us both. "You take a warm bath," she said. "Let that nice smelling lavender soap wash away all the awful things that happened." She kissed her daughter and patted me. "I'll come tuck you in."

ACTIVATE LION MODE

I glanced at my dish as we left the kitchen. I still wasn't hungry. Back in Carolyn's bedroom, I curled up, and went back to sleep.

My bad dreams disturbed the night. Judy lay bleeding, or was it Blade's body? I jerked awake to the crack of a gunshot, or was it the motorhome's body aching as it died alongside the road? I lay awake in the dark listening to Carolyn whimper, and then she lurched upright, her shrill cry piercing my ears.

Mom and Ralph burst into the room. Rushing to opposite sides of the bed, they climbed in and surrounded us in their arms. Carolyn cried, I purred, and Mom hummed a soothing song. Ralph stared out the window, searching the darkness.

CHAPTER TWENTY-FIVE

I woke up too tired to arch my back and stretch. I licked my paws to clean myself, but gave up the effort. At the moment, Carolyn slept soundly although the night had been crowded with her cries and churning limbs. Her angst fed my own. I stared outside. Breaking daylight warmed the birds drinking from the birdbath by the bedroom window. They raised their little heads skyward as water slid down their throats, then ruffled their feathers and splashed in their small concrete pond. Their wings sparkled from the droplets glistening in the morning sun.

In another time, I would have perched on the windowsill, primed for pouncing. I would mimic their chirps and twitch my tail with excitement. Not today. I jumped from the window and padded to the kitchen. Sniffing the uneaten food in my dish, I turned away from it and lapped a little water.

The house was quiet. No boards creaked like they usually did as the sun heated them. The home seemed to hold its breath, waiting. I was tired of waiting, tired of searching, and tired of having adventures with no one to share them. I made my way back down the hall and sprang onto Carolyn's bed. She rolled over, opened her eyes. I meowed hello.

Her hand snaked out from under the covers and scratched my ears. "Hi Cat." I pushed against her palm. Carolyn and I had a bond now. This was as good as any place. I would live out my days here.

The house burst awake. The phone rang at the same time the doorbell chimed, and then chimed again. I jumped from the bed and headed for the front door. Movement and covers rustled from Mom and Ralph's bedroom across the hall. Ralph appeared, shrugging into his robe.

"Who could it be at this time of the morning?" He pulled back the living room drapes and peered out. I squeezed past and leapt onto the window's ledge.

"There he is!" Shouts and flashes erupted outside. A crowd mingled on the lawn. Catching sight of me, they rushed toward the window. Most held video equipment while others flashed their cameras. Ralph slapped the drape shut and stepped to the door. Drawing up to his full height and unlocking the deadbolt, he yanked the thick door open as if it was paper. "What's going on out here?"

The people ignored Ralph and instead, jammed around my window, fighting for a clear photo shot. My curiosity kept me grounded while the group babbled with excitement.

"I said what's going on?" Ralph's face growled. "Get away from the window!"

Ralph's commanding voice caused them to turn. A woman broke from the group and approached him. "Hello, Sergeant Meeker? I'm Nina from Channel 8 news. We heard about how your cat saved the day at one of the biggest busts in human trafficking. Your cat is a hero."

Ralph stared at the reporter, looked at me in the window, and then scanned the entire scene. Three local news vans blocked the driveway. A half a dozen people from various news media milled about in the front yard.

"And your daughter is she home? Your own daughter was rescued from the house of the most dangerous human traffickers in Oregon. Isn't that right?"

From my spot, I watched, as Ralph seemed to arch his back. If he'd had fur like me, it would have stood on end. "All of you, get off my property and go home." He spat out the words. In his bare feet, he herded the glory seekers back to their vehicles.

"But Sergeant Meeker, please! This is a human-interest story. Everyone wants to meet the cat."

Ralph paused and fixed his gaze on the eager reporter. "Look Garcia, give me your card. I'll talk to Carolyn and my wife. But it's seven in the morning. Please, all of you go home."

Garcia fished in his pocket and handed over his card.

Ralph watched the last news van leave, picked up the newspaper on the stoop, and reentered the house. I jumped down from my perch and met him in the kitchen. He turned on the coffeepot, sank into a kitchen chair, and unfolded the paper as Mom entered the room.

"What was that all about?" She rubbed her arms, chilled by the morning, and sat across from Ralph.

Ralph grinned and flipped the newsprint around to her. "It seems we have a famous cat on our hands."

~~JUDY HOWARD~~ SPORTSTER THE CAT

CHAPTER TWENTY-SIX

I leaped up on the table and rubbed up against Mom's arm.

"Hey who said you're allowed on the table?" Ralph reached across the table and scratched my back.

Mom turned the newsprint around to face me. "Look, Cat. You made the front page." Carolyn and Ralph held me in their arms. The white fur on my paws, nose, and chest stood out from the shadowy background where a team of officers huddled. They shouldered shotguns, and posed around Blade, the boyfriend, his dead body hanging halfway out of the limo's open back door.

I rubbed against Mom's hand, which grasped the paper, then moved across the table to Ralph whose fingers cupped his coffee mug. I pushed hard against his arm and the milky brown liquid splashed onto the yellow-laminated tabletop. "Hey, watch it, little fella."

Little fella? Really? I jumped down to the floor, sniffed my bowl, and let out a tiny mew.

"I don't know what's wrong with him," Mom said. "I opened a fresh can, and he still won't eat. I'm getting worried. Maybe we should take him to the vet."

"He's probably fine. Give him a few more days. Last night was pretty stressful." Ralph drew up straight and stretched in his chair. "I guess I'd better get down to the station and finish wrapping up last night's report."

"You want breakfast before you go?" Mom folded the newspaper, laid it down, and wrapped her robe tight as she stood. She jumped when the wall phone rang, and checking the caller ID, her eyes widened. "It's Lois. Oh God, how can I talk to her? She's probably read the headlines."

"I'm sure she just wants to know how Carolyn is." Ralph rinsed his mug in the sink.

"How do I tell her my daughter is safe and sound when Kylie's still missing? "She hugged herself, massaging her shoulders, as the phone rang for the fourth time. "I feel so guilty."

"I'll get it." Ralph took the receiver. "Good morning, Lois. Yes, Carolyn's fine. She had a rough night. She's sleeping in this morning. No, don't worry, you know kids, nothing wakes them. That's a good sign right?" He forced a chuckle. The gesture didn't clear the worry and darkness in his eyes. "Mary's in the shower. I'll tell her you called."

The parents' eyes met as he hung up the phone. "Thank you, honey," Mom said as she began to cry. Ralph wrapped his arms around her. She cried harder as he patted her back.

"It's going to be okay." He ran his hand over her temple and brushed back her mousy hair that had dulled with age. He tipped her chin up. "Carolyn's going to be fine. She's a strong girl."

"It came so close. It could've been like Kylie. I couldn't have faced myself. I should've seen it coming."

"Look. I know you. You'll get through this like you get through everything, by helping others." He kissed her forehead. "Why don't you and Carolyn get dressed and go over to Lois's. Do something positive, like distributing the flyers."

"Why are you crying, Mom?"

Mom pulled back from Ralph, swung around and rushed to her daughter who stood at the kitchen door in her bunny slippers. Gathering her into her arms she said, "Oh, baby. I'm just so relieved you're all right."

Carolyn wiggled out of her mother's embrace and approached Ralph. "I've been thinking. I want to visit Wendy. Can I?"

Ralph looked from his stepdaughter to his wife. Mom's eyes widened with panic. He looked back at Carolyn. "Why do you want to see her?"

ACTIVATE LION MODE

"Well, I've been thinking. Maybe it isn't like what you say. Maybe you're wrong. Or maybe it is like you say. Maybe Wendy wanted to go home, but she couldn't. I just need to see her."

He raised his brows, tilted his head as the corner of his mouth turned down. He looked back at Mom, who could only stare at her daughter. "We'll see, Carolyn. Your mother and I will have to discuss it."

"How about some breakfast?" Mom opened the refrigerator.

"I'm not very hungry."

Mom removed a jug of milk. "At least have a bowl of cereal."

I crouched by my dish and sniffed it again. I understood how Carolyn felt. I couldn't eat either. Carolyn just wanted to know what happened to Wendy like I needed to know what happened to Judy.

I made my way down the hall, curled up on Carolyn's bed, and went back to sleep.

CHAPTER TWENTY-SEVEN

"Wake up, Cat, we're going to see Wendy."

Through a slit in one eye, I peeked over my paw. Carolyn shrugged out of her robe, kicked off her bunny slippers, which landed across the room. She snaked her hips into her jeans. Throwing a t-shirt up and over her raised arms, she wriggled as the garment dropped over her head. Sliding her hands over her tummy, she smoothed out the material, and belly flopped onto the bed, her face inches from mine. "Come on, Cat. You're going, too."

I opened both eyes, raised my head, and looked at her. I couldn't see why I needed to go.

"You can cheer her up. She's gotta be scared. You know how to make a girl feel wanted." She rubbed her face against mine and kissed me.

My body bounced as she jumped off the bed and stood before the mirror. I uncurled, arched my back and stretched. She ran her fingers through her hair, pushing and pulling at wayward strands. I climbed off my pillow and sat in the middle of the bed while she dug through the pile of shoes on the closet floor.

"Mom and Ralph said some reporters are meeting us at Juvie to take your picture. They want to do a story about you." "You're a hero. And we have to go to the veterinarian afterwards, to get you scanned for a chip, to see who you belong to." She whirled around, crouched down by the bedside, and ran her hand over my body and down my tail. "You want to go home, don't you? Anyway, you can't stay with us until we're sure you don't belong to someone."

She jabbered on, but I didn't listen. Sure, I wanted to go home. I've wanted to go home to Judy for a long time, but every time I thought of her, I wanted to howl from the ache. Images of me snug in her lap tugged at my heart, which only made me sadder. I climbed back onto the pillow, my spot still warm.

"Come on, Cat." Carolyn scooped me out of my soft, cozy indentation just as Mom entered with a carrier.

Oh no! I stiffened. I've been this route before. I'm not going back to the place that smelled like death. I wiggled to escape Carolyn's grasp, but she shoved me inside and closed the door.

I howled so loud it reverberated against the cage walls. Carolyn bent down, her face in front of the carrier door. I spat at her and charged the door. She jumped back, startled.

"It's okay, Cat. You're going to be okay." Carolyn's voice quivered. "He doesn't like being in there, Mom. Can't I just hold him?"

Mom patted her daughter's shoulder. "Not in the car. You can take him out when we get there."

I shrank into the recess of the cage as Carolyn carried me to the car. She propped the carrier on her lap as mom climbed in.

The drive didn't take long. I dreaded every minute. I was so tired of everything. I didn't even want to run anymore. I wanted to give up. Judy was probably dead anyway. I pushed that thought from my mind. Cats know things. I may not know where she was, but she wasn't dead. I felt a flicker of hope as images of her crept into my vision. In her lounge chair, she reclined in the shade of a big tree, the motorhome in the background while I lay on her lap and she massaged my back.

I couldn't give up. Judy wouldn't give up on me. I know she wouldn't. Wherever she was, what ever happened to her, she wouldn't stop looking for me. But one thing I knew - I wasn't going back to the pound.

Mom parked in the lot of a large brick building and killed the engine. Carolyn opened the carrier door and, pulling me out, she said, "You can come out now. We're going to visit Wendy. You remember her, don't you?"

ACTIVATE LION MODE

I remembered her. The girl with the cold eyes, but I had recognized a spark in them, too, like an icy flash of evil. It represented Wendy's determined will of survival. You see it in feral cats. They call it the eye of the tiger. Wendy contained ugly experiences hidden in her lithe body, coiled and tight. She was like a racecar with a full tank of nitro. If ignited she would fight, hair on end, back arched, spitting, scratching, and biting. Carolyn saw the fire, too yet she sensed a little girl like herself lived deep inside Wendy, behind the older girl's barbed attitude.

I forgot about my problems and Judy.

We neared the building's entrance when a crowd of people huddled by the door caught sight of us.

"There they are!" They moved like a flock of birds rousted from their perch and swooped around us. Mom drew us close, cradling Carolyn and me with a protective arm just as Ralph poked through the crowd and took a stance beside us.

"Okay, folks. Just a few questions and a few photos." He pointed to Garcia.

Garcia stepped out from the crowd and nodded to Ralph. The reporter's dark hair, dark rimmed glasses, and thick build marked him as Ralph's age. His gentle eyes focused on Carolyn, his voice soft. "Can you tell us in your own words how did this little guy save the day?"

There they go again. Little guy. I'm outta here. I squirmed to get down.

Carolyn held me tighter and said, "If you could stand back a little. You're frightening him."

I wasn't scared, but felt better as the flock shuffled back a few steps.

Carolyn detailed the take down of Blade. "The man had a gun pointed at my head. Cat jumped on his shoulder then climbed up on his baldhead. I saw his back claws rip open his cheek. And Cat bit him in the neck. That's when the man let go of me."

Carolyn's breathing came fast as she relived the scene. "I heard the shot and thought Blade had shot Cat. I was so scared." She rubbed my back and held me to her face, kissing me. "Cat was so brave. He saved my life."

"Someone said he was a stray. Have you found out who he belongs to?"

Ralph stepped forward. "No we haven't. We'll get him scanned for a chip at the veterinarian when he gets his checkup."

Ralph fielded a few more questions, asking how old I was and what kind of cat I was. Someone said I looked like I was part Bengal.

Ralph nodded at an older woman who raised her hand. "Janet."

The woman clutched a notepad and toted a bulging leather bag over her square shoulder. "Carolyn, did you know any of the girls from the sting? Is that why you're here?"

Ralph frowned at Carolyn, "You don't need to answer that, Honey." He focused back on the group. "Let's keep the questions about the cat. We'll take one more."

Carolyn tensed and stepped forward. "No, Ralph. I don't mind." She stood tall with a maturity she hadn't possessed yesterday. "I do have a friend here. Her name is Wendy. She told me she's eighteen, but my dad says she's only fifteen. I think she's like me. She got lured in by these bad people before she knew what was happening. I was lucky." She looked up at Ralph, then down at me, and said, "I don't think she should be in jail. Girls like us don't belong here."

She wiped her eye, ducked back behind her step dad, and whispered. "I want to go see Wendy now."

CHAPTER TWENTY EIGHT

"That's it folks." Ralph herded us past the reporters toward the juvenile hall's entrance.

"Sergeant Meeker! "The older woman shouted out. "This friend of your daughter's? Is she going to be released?" The glass doors swung shut behind us.

At the desk, Ralph pulled out his badge and pointed to me. "I've arranged this with the chief." The officer only glanced at the badge, focusing on Carolyn and me. "Aaah, the famous cat." He nodded at Ralph. "Right this way, Sergeant." We followed him down the hall, where he unlocked the first door. "I'll be right outside," he said as he ushered us inside.

Six chairs tucked around a long table crowded the small room. Wendy sat at one end as if condemned and facing her sentence, her cuffed hands rested in front of her. An orange jumpsuit replaced the designer skinny jeans, and the harsh lights of the interrogation room reflected off her jawline scar. Without makeup, the deformity shouted its gruesome tale of an unspoken moment in the girl's life.

Stripped of her designer disguise, Wendy didn't wilt with embarrassment. She sat, straight-backed, defiant, and glared into Ralph's eyes, which held her challenge without blinking.

ACTIVATE LION MODE

There it was, that spark. I squirmed as Carolyn took her seat, and she released me onto the tabletop. I padded over to Wendy, and stretching up, I rubbed my face against her ugly mark, no longer pink. It was not recent. She jerked her cuffed wrists up to push me away, but paused, and instead, hooked me with her chained hands, and pulled me close. She bowed her head against me, but I leapt from her embrace, escaping across the table. Wendy swallowed hard, straightened, and quickly swiped her damp face with the back of her fists. She focused on me while I made my rounds, from Carolyn, to Mom and then to Ralph. Then she glared back at Ralph.

"Why are you here?" She sneered into his steady brown eyes. "I see you brought the whole family. If you think you've come to rescue me, I don't need it." She twisted in her seat, pounded her clasped fists on the table, and scowled at Carolyn. "I'm eighteen. I don't care what he says. It was just a party. We were just having fun. He murdered my boyfriend."

Ralph shot his own daggered look at Wendy. "I'm here with my family because Carolyn believes in you. She believes you are her good friend and none of the charges against you are valid. She believes you are not a prostitute, and your boyfriend Blade was not a pimp. She believes that you and the other girls were just having a swell old time." He spoke the words slowly, his voice low, his words clipped. "So Carolyn wants to hear it from you. I want her to hear it from you. Tell her."

I lay stretched out on the table, studying Wendy. She dropped her attention back to me. There it was again, that spark. She knew I saw it, and she looked away. She scanned the room, but there was nothing to see but the walls with their scuffs and dents, signatures commemorating way too many tragic, juvenile encounters like this one. Wendy's eyes swung back to me. Her energy charged the air like a caged lion while everyone in the small space held their breath.

Carolyn stood. Her chair scraped the linoleum, and she approached Wendy. She yanked at the empty chair next to Wendy and sat down. Leaning in, elbows on the table, Carolyn propped her chin in her palms. "It's okay, Wendy. Even if it's true, what they say. I'll still be your friend." She nodded to me stretched out on the tabletop. "Me and Cat."

How many ugly moments sliced through the girl's memory in those few seconds? How many could there have been for a fifteen year old? I watched the buried events bubble like lava beneath Wendy's pale complexion.

Carolyn reached up, her finger traced the scarred tissue along her friend's jaw line. "I've always wanted to ask you. How did you get that? It must have really hurt."

Wendy's eyes flared, and before her hot tears erupted, she jumped from her chair, sending it clattering across the room and crashing into the wall. The metal seat scarred the layers of eggshell paint, memorializing the event.

ACTIVATE LION MODE

I smelled Wendy's fear. She kicked the wounded piece of furniture again and it slammed against the barrier. And again, the battered seat etched the emotional action into the wall. The door jerked opened. The guard, poised and ready, shot Ralph a questioning look. . Reading Ralph's imperceptible cue, he tepped back into the hall. The door closed behind him.

No one moved. Mom's forehead creased under the stray locks of hair draping her forehead. Her lips trembled and I thought she might cry. Wendy's deep emotional pain saturated the air. The girl stood staring at the wall, her tense, arched back faced us, her arms rigid, her fists clenched. Carolyn twisted in her seat and glanced at Ralph, who nodded. She rose and crossed the small space to stand by her friend.

"I'm sorry. I shouldn't have asked. You don't have to talk about it." She laced her twelve-year-old fingers with Wendy's and led her shattered friend back to the table. "Here, take my chair." Then she up righted the fallen seat, dragged it next to Wendy, and sat down.

Wendy fiddled with her fingernails. The polish still glittered. Her aura changed and her expression took on an easy smile, almost innocent.

"I used to sit in front of my mirror and put on my mom's make up. My biggest worry was where me and my friends were going to hang out. It was either the mall or the park." She looked over at Carolyn. "Like you were doing when I met you."

I left my place by Mom and Ralph and joined Wendy and Carolyn.

Wendy slid her fingers back and forth over her nail polish. "My mom would never let me wear polish," she said, swallowing hard. Her lips drew into a solemn line, and then her voice lightened. "I used to help her bake cookies."

Carolyn jerked to attention, grabbing her hoodie, and searching a pocket. "I almost forgot," she said. Shooting a glance at Ralph for permission, she pulled a snack bag of Doritos from her pocket. The line of Ralph's lips curled again almost unperceptively and Carolyn's face spread into a big grin. "I don't know what they feed you here..." She said to Wendy and handed her the chips. "They're hot. Your favorite."

Conflicting emotions turned Wendy's face into a battleground. The foray contorted her dry lips and she licked them, and then began chewing on the lower one. Her white-knuckled fingers clutched each other,, as if they clung to the rope of a life preserver. She crossed and uncrossed her ankles. "They feed me fine," she said and took the bag.

The bag crackled as Wendy painted her past. "I worked at the local stable cleaning stalls for three hours to earn an hour of riding time. My favorite horse was a Palomino, I called Trigger. I named him that after watching old western reruns with my folks and my sister." She paused. "My sister must be twelve now."

Now, I really thought she was going to cry. Her eyes grew large. Her heart pounded. She rose and paced the small space. I caught that spark glistening in her eyes. She knotted her fists and her jaw clenched as she gathered control. She stopped next to Ralph and slapped her palms flat on the table. The cuffs clinking against the tabletop. Leaning before him, she brought her face close to his. "Blade's dead?"

Empathy for the girl with the cold eyes clouded Ralph's and he scowled. I knew he wouldn't cry but he blinked and cleared his throat. "He can't hurt you anymore."

Wendy straightened, went back to her seat, and slid into her chair. The fifteen-year-old girl who looked eighteen focused her hard cold eyes on Carolyn's.

"I'm fifteen and I'm a prostitute. Blade was my pimp."

~~JUDY HOWARD~~ SPORTSTER THE CAT

CHAPTER TWENTY-NINE

"The shrinks call it the honeymoon period," Wendy's intense eyes locked into Carolyn's which blinked hesitantly. "Isn't that the way you felt with Blade?"

Carolyn sat up straighter, her face brightened. "I knew you'd understood. He was so nice. I think he loved me ... a lot."

Wendy raised her hand, shushing Carolyn. "I met Blade at the mall at Barney's or Hot Topic, some store like that. My friends and me were checking out the new shipment of jeans that none of us could afford. Every weekend we got together, hung out, and bitched that our folks wouldn't buy us nice clothes and about how they were always telling us what we could and couldn't do.

"Maybe it was Macy's. Blade had been watching from a distance, watching just me. He would shoot me a big smile and nod when I held up a pair, pinned them against me, and swung my hips around like a model. He was into me. Not my friends, but just me."

Wendy peered over Carolyn and Mom and glanced at Ralph. His eyes softened and he gave her the slightest nod of encouragement. She dropped her gaze, wringing her hands. "We met every chance I could sneak away from home. He gave me heroin so I could get high. I started skipping school and my parents came down even harder on me. I only hated them more. Blade bought me designer jeans, took me to fancy restaurants, and even got me backstage at concerts. He told me I was his little Barbie. So when he said I could come stay with him, I was thrilled. I moved in. I was going to show my parents."

Carolyn placed her hands over Wendy's white knuckled fists. "I'm sorry. I didn't know you were together. I never meant to …."

"You don't understand, girl." Wendy jerked her hands away from Carolyn's sympathetic touch. "He was just spitting the game."

Carolyn's forehead creased. "Spitting the game?"

"Yeah. He was building my trust, grooming me. That's how the shrinks explain it. I've been to a few, who tried to rescue me, but I wouldn't listen. Why should I? Blade loved me. He gave me everything I wanted. At first it was fine, then, all of a sudden, it wasn't."

Carolyn's mouth hung open. She shifted in her chair, scanned the room, passing over her mother's worried look. I guessed she wished she could leave.

Wendy pushed up from the table and began pacing, focusing on nothing. She concentrated on her past with new eyes.

"He took me to his apartment and introduced me to a twenty year old girl named Tanya and said she was his girlfriend. I was shocked. Up until then I had every reason to believe he had fallen head over heels in love with me. I was embarrassed and angry. I told him I wanted to go home. His fist sank into my stomach so hard and fast I couldn't breathe. I passed out from the pain."

Tears flowed from Carolyn's eyes as they tracked her friend, pacing back and forth.

"Blade took Tanya and me to the Marriot and told us there was a man waiting in a room upstairs. We were to do whatever the guy asked. Again, I begged to go home and he promised if I would just do this for him …if I loved him I would do it for him … then he would take me home." Wendy slumped back into her chair. "That was three years ago. I never went home."

"After that…that time … I argued with Blade because he wouldn't take me home. He beat me and forced himself on me. He withheld my heroin until I cramped up from withdrawals. My body began to shake and I didn't want to be touched, but he forced himself on me anyway, to teach me a lesson, he said.. That was when he liked it most."

ACTIVATE LION MODE

Mom jumped up and rushed to her daughter's side. "Come on, honey. You've heard enough."

Carolyn allowed her mother to drag her out of her chair. Trance-like Carolyn stood, then looked at me. She swooped me up and cradled me.

The room smelled thick with ugliness, sadness, and a hopelessness. I rubbed against Carolyn's neck and purred as loudly as I could. I thought of my time in the pound with Snowy Cat and her kittens, I thought of Judy. I wanted to go home, too.

Carolyn's face twisted and she buried it against Mom's chest. Her young-girl tears dropped, wetting my fur. I shook my head.

Wendy pounded her cuffed wrists against the table and the loud rapping interrupted Carolyn's shocked silence. The girl who looked eighteen fixed her gaze on the girl who had proclaimed to be her friend. "It's okay. You can leave. I get it."

Carolyn looked from her mom to Wendy and back again as she fought her opposing feelings.

Mom herded us toward the door. "Come on, Honey. We can come back and visit, again." Nodding, Carolyn looked at the ground as Ralph knocked on the door, alerting the guard in the hall. I peered back when we exited. Wendy sat, her hands covering her face. Now she looked fifteen.

***

The dark mood clung to the family, following them to waiting room. Mom and Carolyn stared at the floor. Ralph put an arm around Carolyn and me and steered us toward the door. "Come on Baby, Let's go home."

Outside Ralph growled at the few reporters still mingling and waving them away said, "Back off." Inside the car, Mom laid her hand on Ralph's knee as he started the engine. "I got a text from the veterinarian. He canceled because of an emergency surgery. I rescheduled for Monday. Cat gets a couple more days with Carolyn."

Ralph nodded and pulled out of the parking lot while I huddled in the backseat in Carolyn's arms hoping no one realized I wasn't in the cage.

A sprinkle of reporters lined the sidewalk when we arrived at the house. Again, Ralph shooed them back, "Please folks. I'll give a statement to the press Monday afternoon, after the cat's vet appointment."

"Sergeant, how is your daughter? We understand she visited her friend at Juvenile Hall. What will happen to her friend?" Janet, the older reporter from yesterday morning fingered a wayward grey strand of hair and tucked it in with the rest tied to the side of her neck with a bright purple ribbon

ACTIVATE LION MODE

"No more questions, Janet. It's been a long morning." Ralph paused before turning to go inside. "I'm getting in touch with the correct agencies which deal with victims of prostitution and trafficking. By Monday I'll have more to report."

***

The Meeker family passed the rest of the day crouched down within the safety of their home. Mom fixed sandwiches for lunch and refreshed my dish with a new flavor of fishy smelling food. "Linda across the street gave me this. She says her cat loves it."

I sniffed the mixture, licked it a couple of times. I wasn't hungry. I padded back to my spot by the kitchen door.

Ralph shoved potato chips in his already full mouth and said, "I'm sure he's fine. He probably wants to go home."

Mom bent down and picked me up, hugging me. "What's the matter little guy? I'll bet you have a nice mommy somewhere who is worried sick about you."

Carolyn rose from her chair, leaned in and kissed me. "I want to keep you, Cat. I love you. But I know how important it is to go home."

We finished the day napping and watching movies. Ralph periodically checked on the reporters' vigil in the front yard. Two vehicles remained Garcia's and Janet's. "Those two are like the old coon hounds my grandpa had in Alabama. Those dogs would track 'til they dropped." The drape fell back across the window and Ralph surveyed his family. Carolyn slept with her head on Mom's lap while Mom worked a crossword puzzle. The TV droned softly, flashing shadowy ghosts into the room. I perched on the back of the sofa.

He picked up the remote, the room darkened, the ghosts receded, and a silence settled in. "It's been a long day. Let's pack it in." He lifted Carolyn off the couch.

"Be careful, Ralph. Your back."

"There won't be many more times I'll get to do this, and I don't mean because of my back."

Mom smiled up at him. She set her puzzle aside and turned off the lamp. I watched the Meeker family disappear down the hall.

In the darkness, a familiar, crystalline voice drifted from the radio in Janet's vehicle. ....*I know I could never cry your tears, but I would if I could...* Judy loved Celine, and this song in particular. When Judy sang the words to me, I had believed she would always be there for me. But now?

I curled into a tight ball and tucked my nose under my paws. I slept until the haunting images of Judy's body lying on the ground beside our motorhome woke me. I jumped down from the couch and hopped up on the windowsill. The dome light in Janet's Expedition illuminated the streaks of her grey hair. *...if I could... I would protect your innocence from time....if I could....*Janet couldn't sleep either. I wondered what her story was.

~~JUDY HOWARD~~ SPORTSTER THE CAT

CHAPTER THIRTY

"You've got to see this!" Carolyn burst into her parents' bedroom with the morning paper, and squeezing between them, sat cross-legged. . "Look! Cat's on the front page!"

Mom reached for her reading glasses as Ralph fluffed the pillows and sat up.

This was no time to be aloof. I jumped up and joined them. A close up of me in Carolyn's arms captured my courageous nature. I was amazed how the black and white photo caught the spark in my eyes. My depression lightened as I gazed at myself. Mom pushed up onto her elbows, took the paper, and read aloud.

"They just call him Cat. A simple name for a Hero. Last night Cat's clever actions were crucial in the take down of a well-organized human trafficking ring. During a city wide sting operation, Portland PD's Human Trafficking Unit killed a key player, Dennis Paris, aka King Blade, and identified and arrested nineteen other known sex traffickers ... but not without the help of Cat..... Details in Local Section, page 9.

The paper rustled as Mom thumbed through the pages to the featured story titled, *A hero named Cat.*

ACTIVATE LION MODE

Finishing the piece, Mom folded the news piece and studied me perched in Carolyn's lap. "Well, aren't you the celebrity?" Ralph petted me I puffed out my chest and purred loudly.

Interrupted by the phone's shrill ring, my proud moment was short lived. Ralph checked his watch. "Who can that be at seven on a Saturday morning?" He stretched across Mom and grabbing the receiver. "Meeker residence." He nodded to the voice on the other end of the line, listened, and nodded, again. When he hung up, he smiled at me. "Well Cat, your fans are beating the door down at the precinct. There's a crowd at the station, folks willing to take you in if we don't find your owner. Folks are donating stuffed animals, cat treats, and even a kitty condo in the spirit of your hero status."

I was never into all that fancy stuff. Just give me a twisty tie, rubber band, or a crumpled wad of paper. I rolled over, exposing my belly for Carolyn to rub.

"The desk officer is texting us contact information for a couple who claim Cat looks like a stray they adopted from the pound five days ago. They live two blocks over from us."

Carolyn sat up. "Oh, so they're the owners?"

"They adopted him. So yes, I guess so." Mom said.

"But if he came from the shelter, he must have had a home before that," Carolyn said. "They aren't his real parents."

Ralph threw back his bedcovers and climbed out of bed. "We'll find out just who he really belongs to. I'm afraid we might have a slew of folks who would do anything to own a famous cat." He smiled down at me and patting me on the head. "Don't worry, Cat. They didn't pin detective stripes on me for nothing."

Everyone went about their morning business while I curled up in the bed covers and tried to go back to sleep. My mind drifted to a time when I lay in Judy's bed in our motorhome, stretched out and purring, while Judy fussed with her morning chores. Outside our motorhome window, I would catch sight of some animal - a rabbit, a deer, even a turkey once, rustling around our campsite, enjoying the morning's solitude before campers and their dogs disturbed their habitat.

How many hours had I spent staring out the window, dreaming of what it would be like to be free like them? I envied the creatures' abandon to sniff every rock, every bush, and to chase whatever bug or butterfly crossing their path. Back then, I longed to live in the wild.

The excitement of the forest was like a she-cat calling. So when my wish came true, I greeted the adventure with the innocence of a young tom. But I never wanted it at the expense of losing Judy. How could I have known I would never see her again?

ACTIVATE LION MODE

Ralph's booming voice sang backup to the shower's musical spray while forest images filled my head. I licked my paws, washed my face and then shook my head as I remembered how the ferns tickled my ears. I had padded deep into my pine-carpeted new world, drinking dew drops, and marking my scent while I followed intriguing scents along the trodden paths, worn down by unfamiliar creatures. I was living the life. I thought I didn't need Judy.

Things changed quickly. I did not account for the bear whose breath was as deadly as his claws or the creature with horns reaching to the sky. Living in the wild meant no warm bed, no Fancy Feast, and no private bathroom. Like Wendy, it didn't take long before I wanted to go home. Living the life came with a big price. A price did not want to pay.

Am I a hero? I don't think so. After the second day of living the life, I was afraid, hungry, and I missed Judy desperately. Carolyn is lucky. She got to go home.

SPORTSTER THE CAT

CHAPTER THIRTY-ONE

Haunting memories kept me from sleeping. I padded down the hall to the noises in the kitchen as Ralph came up behind me. He kissed Mom on the back of her neck and grabbed a mug off the counter. "The couple is Mellie and Richard Romero," he said. "They're on their way over. They adopted Mittens, that's what they named him, last Sunday." He poured a cup of coffee. "They're bringing another cat they named Snow White, which they adopted at the same time. It seems Cat was friends with Snow, who had four kittens. They must be nice people to take in two strays and four kittens."

Mom and Carolyn exchanged worried expressions in response to the knock on the door. I raced to the front windowsill and peered out. It was Mellie and Richard, all right. Richard carried a cage. My heartbeat jumped. No one was taking me back to the pound. I remained on the windowsill, behind the curtain, as Ralph opened the door and everyone introduced themselves.

"And this is Snow White." Mellie kneeled down and opened the cage door. "I'm sure Mittens will remember her." The cat from the carrier glided out like a cottony cloud floating on a breeze. Her downy feathery fur skimmed the tile in the foyer. I peeked out past the curtain and chirped, "Miss Snow?" She chirped and turned to me as I leapt from the sill and trotted over to her. She was beautiful. And happy. I could see that. She had helped to fill the void Katie's death had left for Mellie and Richard.

I purred loudly, rubbing against first Mellie's ankles and then Richard's. Snow began licking her pristine paws. I wondered what became of her kittens but confident Mellie and Richard had found them good homes. I had worried about Snow, but now I found a bit of peace knowing I had aided her escape from the claws of that mangy gang banger, Blackie, at the shelter.

Ralph removed himself from our little reunion when the phone rang again.

"They seem to recognize one another," Carolyn said as she ran her hand over Snow's soft snowy coat. "But I want to know who had him before he came to the shelter."

Mellie squatted down alongside Carolyn and ran her hand over my back. "The man at the pound said an elderly couple brought him in because he was a stray and he had bit the man." She bent down and kissed me. "He does have a feisty side. We almost didn't adopt him because he hissed and growled at us." She beamed at me." But we got past that didn't we Mittens?"

"Well, I'm grateful he has a courageous attitude. My Carolyn might not be here today if it wasn't for Cat." Mom said.

Mellie stood up. "I know what you mean Mrs. Meeker. I want to believe this cat was there to help my Katie make her transition. Mittens will always be special to us." The two women hugged, and Mellie wiped a tear away as Ralph reentered the room.

"It seems we have another complication," Ralph said as he stood beside his wife and gazed down at Carolyn and the two cats. "That was a gentleman named Armando Ramos on the phone. He's a student at the university. He claims he and a fellow veteran buddy …," Ralph glanced at the slip of paper in his hand, "… Patrick Salas were camping in the Olympic forest near the town of Forks last week. Cat came into the campsite and made himself at home. They want to come by and see if it is the same cat."

Mellie and Richard's eyes met while Carolyn studied their reaction to the new twist. "When will they be here?" Richard asked. He reached out and linked his arm around his wife's back, pulling her close.

"They said they can be here in an hour."

Mom drew herself up and wrung her hands. "Look, why don't you two come on into the kitchen and have a cup of coffee while we wait. We're practically neighbors." She herded my family, which was increasing in size by the hour, into the kitchen. "So how long have you lived in Portland?"

They left Snow and me to ourselves. She went back into her carrier, curled up and went to sleep. I

ACTIVATE LION MODE

returned to my post on the windowsill and waited for the next phase of my past to unfold.

~~JUDY HOWARD~~ SPORTSTER THE CAT

CHAPTER THIRTY-TWO

I recognized the pinging and clunking as the truck parked at the curb. The steady rhythmic voices in the kitchen chattered away while I peeped a tiny chirp to myself. I almost didn't recognize Guitarman. His long legs poked out from the vehicle and he stood, towering over the cab. The long, greasy strands he had the habit of constantly shoving from his eyes were free and curling out from his dusty knit cap. His hair was shorter, his curls tighter.

Tattooman scooted out on the passenger side and began to shut the door when a dog, perched on the seat, began to bark in protest of being left. "I'll be back. You wait here."

It was Jawbreaker! His familiar bark touched my heartstrings as Tattooman slammed the door and joined his buddy.

I jumped from the windowsill and sprinted into the foyer as Ralph opened the door to the veteran's knock. Bolting past the forest of legs, I dashed to the truck and sprang onto the hood. Catching sight of me, Jawbreaker broke into a song of fevered barking. I plopped by butt down in front of the windshield and stared at him. He pranced on the seat, yipping and whining, and licking the glass in an attempt to kiss me.

I switched my tail and shot an expectant stare back at the stunned men on the porch. I twitched it again.

"I guess he's the cat." Guitarman grinned at Ralph. "I named him Ka-Bar."

Ralph pointed to the reunion. "You'd better let the dog out, before he tears up your truck. What's his name?"

"We call him Pit." He paused, faced Ralph, and reached out his hand. "And I'm Armando Ramos, sir, and this is my buddy, Patrick Salas. You must be Sergeant Meeker?"

"Call me Ralph." Ralph clasped Guitarman's hand and shook it.

"Yes, sir, Ralph, sir," Guitarman and Armando said.

Tattooman, or Armando, also shook Ralph's hand. "Good to meet you, sir." Guitarman strode back to the truck, and before he opened the door half way, Jawbreaker scrambled out.

I moved to the fender's edge, as the dog danced on his hind legs and wailed, "I love you."

~~JUDY HOWARD~~ SPORTSTER THE CAT

I ended Jawbreaker's embarrassing display of emotion and leaped to the ground. He slobbered me with kisses while I weaved back and forth through his legs, butting my head against his. He planted his elbows flat on the sidewalk, his rear in the air and his tail curled. His tail wagged back and forth like the windshield wipers in a downpour. I rolled over and exposed my belly. He dove in, burying his nose in my furry tummy, and nudged me around as if I were a toy.

The three men stood in a half circle, observing our reunion. "You're right," Ralph said. "He's the cat. But we have a problem."

Tattooman and Guitarman switched their attention from our happy homecoming and focused on the Ralph's declaration. Tattooman resembled his dog. His sheer bulk propped his arms away from his sides, probably from many hours in the gym, while Guitarman reminded me of Judy's string mop that propped in the corner of the laundry room at home.

Ralph raised his heavy brows and nodded toward the house. "There's a couple inside who claim they adopted Cat last week."

The two veterans exchanged solemn looks.

"We have a dilemma, gentlemen," Ralph said. "Your Ka-Bar, or who we call, Cat, and who the couple named Mittens - whatever his name is --definitely knows us all."

ACTIVATE LION MODE

The men stared at Ralph.

Ralph raised his brows and grinned. "Why don't you come in? Let's all have some coffee, see if we can untangle this mess. Bring the dog, too."

Guitarman snapped on Jawbreaker's leash, and they all stalked into the house. I padded past the new additions to my family and led the stiff parade into the kitchen.

Ralph made the introductions while Mom prepared another pot of coffee. , Carolyn, brooded with uncertainty as she sat next to Mellie and Richard. The young girl's fingers tapped a steady rhythm on her cell, but periodically her nervous eyes rolled up to study the new participants involved in my past.

"Gentlemen, have a seat," Ralph said. "I'll get more chairs."

Tattooman ordered Jawbreaker to scoot under his chair.

After a quick pass by my dish, reassured the dog hadn't touched my food, I took my usual position and crouched by the doorway, leading into the hall.

Served with coffee and a slice of Mom's blackberry cobbler, the group settled in. Mom sank into the seat beside Carolyn, and they both gazed up to the two men. "So, tell us how you gentlemen met Cat," Mom said.

The two chuckled, recalling my infiltration of their camp. Guitarman, or Patrick as everyone was calling him, unwound his slight build, peered down at me and said, "He came at a low point in my life." Out of habit, he swiped a shag of hair that no longer hung over his eyes and then he squinted. He and Armando's eyes met. "You had, Pit," Patrick said, "and I envied you,"

Armando set his jaw then stared at the tabletop.

"When Ka-Bar came along it was obvious he was as lost and as lonely as I was." Patrick-Guitarman raised his brow. "The little guy took to me. He needed me." He scratched his chin and the lank man focused on me again and shook his head. "I don't see how a cat could make such a difference, but he did."

I trotted over and rubbed against his leg.

Tattooman, or Armando, looked across the room as if lost in a memory, yet nodded as he listened. Guitarman leaned back in his chair and smiled at his buddy, "Remember the hurt Ka-Bar put on Pit when they first met? And, Pit forgave him. Pit knows the cat is special, too."

I sprang up into Carolyn's lap. She drew me close and nuzzled me. Mellie and Richard recounted their encounter.

"So after he left you guys," Carolyn said, "He must have ended up with the people who claimed he bit them, and they took him to the shelter." Carolyn's foot made tapping sounds on the floor. Carolyn shot a smirk at Mellie and Richard. "Wouldn't the shelter check for a chip?"

"They're supposed to..." Richard said quickly, then his words trailed off, and he fidgeted with his spoon.

Mellie's forehead creased. "We assumed they did and they didn't find any identification."

They all exchanged glances. Each nodded slowly.

Richard shot a challenging look to the group. "So now the cat should have a chip denoting us as his owners, don't you think? We should have received paperwork about the chip, but we didn't. I suppose it was an error on the shelter's part. They were very busy that day."

Ralph, in detective mode, took control.

"At his veterinary appointment they will check for a chip. I've arranged a news conference Monday at noon," Ralph said. "Cat's public wants to know what becomes of him. I'll announce then who the owner is. So for now, he stays here with Carolyn."

They all remained silent, lost in their own thoughts.

Guitarman's brow furrowed and the slim guitar player mumbled to no one in particular, "Ka-Bar and Pit love each other."

Richard's brows knitted. He rubbed his temple. "I think Snowy and Mittens were a couple and they seem to love each other, too."

The tension in the air was thick. I made my rounds, head butting each of my concerned family members. Guitarman clamped his fists. I paused, purring and brushing against his clenched hands. Exhaling, shoved away from the table. "Let's go," he said to his dog and Pit scrambled out from under the table.

I moved over to Carolyn and she tugged me close, wrapping her arms around me.

Carolyn lifted her chin. "So if there's no ID, what will we do?"

The group leaned back in their seats, fixing their gaze on Ralph. Ralph looked to Carolyn who continued to hug me, kissing and reassuring me, everything would be okay. They all studied the scene for a moment and then, saying no more, left.

ACTIVATE LION MODE

CHAPTER THIRTY-THREE

Ralph and Mom showed everyone to the door while I followed Carolyn to her room and curled up beside her on the bed. I spent the afternoon and evening, as well as the next day, sleeping. Images of Judy and the places we'd visited floated in my mind. The roar of Niagara Falls' roar boomed in my ears and the misty vision of New York filled my vision. I opened my eyes only to close them again when I realized I was not in our motorhome with my Judy. I revisited the scenes of New York, the Stature of Liberty and Ground Zero, and Washington DC's proud heritage. The Pentagon Memorial and Arlington were all just memories now, like Judy.

The sensation of soaring through the air as I leaped toward a bird felt so real the excitement woke me. But it was Carolyn's hands sliding around me, grasping me, and lifting me up. By the time I became fully awake she had already shoved me in that hated carrier. I squalled.

"It's okay, Cat. You have to go to the doctor." Carolyn flipped the latch. My protests upset her, I could tell.

I bawled with every bit of air in my lungs. She glanced up at Mom who stood in the doorway. 'He'll be fine, Honey. Come on. Ralph's waiting in the car."

I was not fine. I howled all the way.

They carried me into the building that smelled like antiseptic. Mews, and howls, barking and Death bounced off the walls. I howled even louder.

Carolyn held the cage on her lap and sat between Mom and Ralph. I convinced her to be as upset as me.

"Can I take him out? He hates being in there."

Ralph nodded to a sign on the wall. "It says they must be restrained. Anyway as upset as he is, I don't think you should."

My relentless protest resulted in a sterile smelling girl who ushered us deeper into the caverns. She motioned to an examination room and Carolyn shuffled in, setting my carrier on a metal table. The girl bent down and smiled, sticking her finger in the cage door. "It's going to be okay, Cat."

I screamed at her and my paws pounded the mesh grate. She jumped away before I could bite her finger.

"Oh dear, he's really upset. The doctor will be right in." Spinning around, her back straight and elbows tight against her body, she scurried out of the room.

ACTIVATE LION MODE

The medicine odors combined with my adrenaline made me heave. I hadn't eaten in days so only yellow bile pooled on the cage floor.

The doctor, smelling like everything else in this place, stepped into the room, I belted out my loudest roar ever.

"So this is the famous Cat?" He bent down and peered in at me. I screamed at him, too, struck at the grate, and at the same time, jumped up, hoping the ceiling would give way. The carrier bounced and rattled against the stainless steel examine table. I growled, hissed. Mom, Carolyn and Ralph huddled in the corner.

I thought I'd convinced the man not to mess with me, because he stepped towards the door, as the girl had done. But he only whispered to someone in the hall and in a moment, the young girl joined him.

The doctor and girl said nothing to one another, as they began unscrewing the clasps that held the top of the carrier. Good. They're going to let me out. A sliver of daylight lit up the interior as the cage top rose. I'm out of here. I spun around with a growl and hiss to make my retreat, but not before a painful prick shot into my back leg. Anger seared through me like the slash of a claw. I bellowed out my last screech. A heaviness flooded through me. I had been betrayed. Death seized me. My life force faded from me. I couldn't hear my own last roar. Everything went black.

~~JUDY HOWARD~~ SPORTSTER THE CAT

CHAPTER THIRTY-FOUR

Voices floated in my foggy brain. I lifted my heavy eyelids. Still trapped. I sniffed the floor of my carrier. Someone had cleaned up the yellow bile and wiped the goo from my fur. My tongue, thick and dry, stuck to my paw as I licked it, and when I meowed, my voice cracked. The scent of water in the cup hanging on the grate lured me to stand. Shaking legs barely held me upright. Leaning against the cage wall, I lapped up every drop then collapsed.

The urgency of my situation caused my mind to race. I had to escape this coffin of death, but my eyes drooped, and I dozed off again. Disjointed words penetrated my senses. "Judy...in Southern California.....a dead phone line ..."

I must have slept through my press conference. I awoke more clear headed, but still in the cage. The door stood ajar! I sprang for the opening, pushed past the grate, but only stumbled out. I found myself in Carolyn's bedroom. I dashed for safety under the bed and looked back, my heart pumping. I had escaped the cage of death. Carolyn was not in her room, but conversations filtered down the hall from the kitchen. My legs trembled as I sprinted down the corridor, staying close to the wall for support. I peered into the kitchen.

"I've got a buddy who's a Riverside Sheriff Detective. We know Cat's owner is a woman called Judy Howard, but we just don't know where she is."

Judy? I chirped, shuffled into the kitchen, and sprang for the tabletop. But I misjudged and fell back to the floor. I shook it off, sat down, and decided to listen from where I sat by Carolyn.

Mom sat between her daughter and Ralph. "The guy at the pound admitted he'd been distracted when he was supposed to scan Cat for his chip," Mom said. "Everyone assumed he had checked, and that there was no chip."

"I wonder what happened to this Judy. Portland is a long way from Southern California." Carolyn said.

Judy! There! I heard her name again. I jumped into Carolyn's lap.

"Oh there you are, Cat." Carolyn hugged me. "You were so upset at the doctor's. I see you're feeling better."

What about Judy? What do you know? Is she okay? I rubbed against Carolyn and purred loudly. I skirted across the table and butted my head against Ralph's hand.

"Hey buddy, watch it." He pushed me away as his coffee splashed onto his dinner roll and last bite of mashed potatoes. "Careful. You'll get burned. I know you don't want to go back to the veterinarian."

Ralph sopped up the spilt caffeine with a paper towel, and tossed it onto his plate. Bending down, he kissed Mom. "I've gotta get going," He called over his shoulder, as he gathered up his gear from the laundry room. "Did I tell you Wendy's turning state witness? Her testimony's making a solid case for the D.A."

"Can Cat and I visit her again? I want her to know how much I care."

Ralph stepped back in the kitchen and patted me on the head. "I'll see what I can do, Pumpkin."

Ralph went out the door. What about Judy?

As the screen door slammed shut, Mom wiped her mouth and rose to answer the phone. She listened for a moment, smiled, and said, "Sure, I remember you. Nursing school wouldn't have been the same without you, Paula. I never would have graduated without all our midnight cramming sessions. How are you?"

After another moment Mom said," How about Sergio's? Tomorrow at noon?"

She paused a moment. "The cat? How did you know about the cat?"

ACTIVATE LION MODE

Carolyn looked up, forehead creased, and listened closely. Mom met her gaze, raised her brows, and shrugged at her daughter.

"Yes we still have him, but how...?" Mom shrugged again. "We're trying to locate his owner." She grinned. "No, he's not going anywhere yet. Tomorrow at Sergio's. See you then."

Mom hung up the receiver, returned to the table. "That was my dear friend, Paula. We went to nursing school together. She works in Washington at the Forks Community Hospital."

"What's wrong? What did she want? Why did she ask about Cat?"

"She wants to meet for lunch tomorrow when she visits her sister who lives here in Portland."

"What did she say about Cat?"

"Cat made the news up there, too." Mom wiped down the counter, deep in thought. "Paula says she'll explain it all at lunch. Clear the table, please. Did you call for the assignments you've missed? You've got a lot of homework to catch up on."

I followed Carolyn back down the hall, but balked at her bedroom door. The cage of death remained in the middle of the room. I escaped to the living room and hid behind the curtains, crouching and trembling. I had to make a plan. The talk of Judy stirred me with hope. She must be close. I needed to continue my trek. I knew I would be safe if I could just find her.

ACTIVATE LION MODE

CHAPTER THIRTY-FIVE

The house was dark, quiet except for an occasional creak. A sliver of moonshine slipped through the small opening in the curtains and created a light bar on the carpet. The muffled swish of a car moving down the street was the only sound. I waited. I crept from my hiding place and headed down the hall. My legs were steady again. I glanced in Mom and Ralph's bedroom. Only Mom. Ralph would be home soon.

I froze at Carolyn's door. My back arched and my hair stood on end. That diabolical cage of death remained on the floor in the middle of the room. Like a predator, it waited. My tail twitched. The standoff continued. I crouched, my eyes fixed on my steadfast prey. When Ralph's car pulled in the drive, I dashed to escape out the back door when it opened.

I hit the kitchen tile on the run, a direct route for the door, but it closed quickly. I braked, but unable to stop, I slid. Banking against Ralph's leg, I propelled in the reverse direction, coming to a halt in the hallway.

"Hey! What's up, Cat?" He laid his gear on the washing machine and then pulled a container from the fridge and a fork from a drawer. As he sank into a chair, I leaped onto the table and nudged his hand.

"What's up, Cat? Can't sleep?" He scratched my head, his fingers working their way down my back. I purred. I liked Ralph's steadiness, as if no matter what went wrong, everything would work out, but I don't think he understood about the cage of Death or he would not have allowed it in the house.

He finished the leftover spaghetti, rinsed the container and his fork, and then lumbered down the hall. I waited until he whispered a greeting to Mom and disappeared into the bedroom. Trotting to my post behind the curtains, on the windowsill, I took up my surveillance. The full moon lit up the sky, reminding me of a similar night when I took my leave of Guitarman, Tatooman, and Jawbreaker. That night seemed ages ago.

My tail flicked back and forth, recalling the thrill of living in the wild in the Olympic forest. My heart pulsed. It was the time of my life, exotic scents, musical bird songs and the insects' buzz. I had activated lion mode.

My ears telescoped around to catch soft giggles floating from the closed bedroom door, then silence again.

The thrills, the adventure, the freedom of living free made my heart race, even now.

When I had met Jawbreaker's sad eyes and said goodbye on a moonlit night like tonight, magic filled the heavens, or maybe it was only the excitement of being on my own, taking risks, and making my own decisions.

Although the air had only smelled of the fairground's asphalt, it promised coming adventures. And freedom!

I chirped a tiny meow. Adventures and freedom … and sacrifice. This sky, drenched in quiet moonlight, was like then. The illusion pulled me. I had left those who cared about me. Now, I will make the same move, again. I needed Judy.

~~JUDY HOWARD~~ SPORTSTER THE CAT

CHAPTER THIRTY-SIX

The hustle in the kitchen woke me, but not before the screen door slammed shut and the house returned to its whispering creaks and moans. I had slept too late. I was alone with the Cage of Death. I prowled around in the laundry room and by the front door, looking for a way outside. My hope dwindled, and I returned to my surveillance on the windowsill. I would wait until the family came home for dinner. It was going to be a long day, but the Cage of Death seemed content to wait for me to come to it. That was not going to happen.

***

Once I renewed my quest, days might pass before I ate again. I wandered into the kitchen and nibbled the fresh tuna in my dish. During my crusade, I had mastered the art of hunting for food. Handouts would be easy. Folks are suckers for purring, head butts, and belly exposing antics. I also had learned not to allow any sweet smelling, long haired She-Cat to trick me. There will be no more Annabelle's in my life to spit her game and take me prisoner at a shelter.

Living free had its price. In the wild, no one would be there to watch my back. I had to activate lion mode.

No one would be around to comfort me and no one would rely on me either. At home, Judy needed me. I missed that most. She depended on me to wake her in the morning. Sometimes she acted shy and counted on me to introduce her to fellow campers. I kept her warm during the cold nights. I wondered what she was doing now.

Sure, the good people I met along my journey depended on me, too. Guitarman and I had shared a bond. Each of us had been lost and alone, but he and Tattoman had found their way. It was time for me to do the same.

My mind drifted to my little friend Katie. Walking alongside her on her journey to another place and time had refueled my lagging spirit.

Now, there was Carolyn. She is so young and vulnerable. I will never forget her either.

Being free? That's just some people talking. I've realized my prison is prowling through this world all alone. Where have I heard that before? My paws are cold at night and my heart is always hungry. I want to go home. I can't give up my search.

Exhaust fumes seeped under the door as Mom's car pulled into the carport. The side door opened and Carolyn burst into the laundry room. I bolted past her before the door slammed shut, but froze, my tail almost became crushed in the jam. A familiar scent stunned me.

SPORTSTER THE CAT

In the carport, Mom bent over the car's trunk, fumbling with her purse as she retrieved shopping bags. A light fragrance floated to my nose like a feather. The aroma wafted past me, carried away by the breeze. It was Judy!

I rushed toward Mom and jumped into trunk. The ghostly fragrance vanished. I inspected everything, first the trunk, and then Mom. It had been ever so faint. I couldn't be sure.

Judy had to be close. I scanned the yard and the carport. No Judy. I had mixed feelings. Should I follow the scent or wait? A leader must be able to make snap decisions. Judy said that once.

Search!

I sprinted through the bushes and into the street. I veered to the right to avoid the vehicle looming toward me. The screech of tires and its blaring horn startled me. Fire bit into my shoulder, and I rolled like a tumbleweed. Images spun in my brain. I howled and clawed for a foothold. Dizziness overcame me.

Trembling, my limp body came to a rest in the gutter but pain and panic spurred me to get up, seek shelter. The park wasn't far. I sprinted off down the sidewalk, but stumbled when my front leg gave out. My chin scraped the concrete. I shook my head to clear it and rose again, limping and crawling, until I reached the green grass and bushes in the park. An opening under a large rock, hidden in a clump of foliage caught my eye, and I crawled toward it. Tunneling into the cavern, I hunkered down, gritting my teeth to stop their chattering.

The trembling would not stop, and I threw up. When the heavy, shudders finally lessened, a lightness lifted me up and away from the throbbing ache in my shoulder. The pounding in my brain faded, and my eyelids drooped. I exhaled, drifting into my sweet lion's den where there was no pain, no fear, and no loneliness.

~~JUDY HOWARD~~ SPORTSTER THE CAT

CHAPTER THIRTY-SEVEN

The day drifted by like a dream until shadows overtook the park. Voices floated, echoing in the deep den of darkness, which cradled me.

"Here, Cat! Come on, Cat."

I lifted my head. Pain pierced my shoulder and my chin dropped onto my paw. Thoughts of home floated in my head as the stabbing discomfort intensified. I attempted to move again, but a cold stiffness prevented me. I sank back into the pillow of sleep.

Sunlight filtered through the bushes and I blinked. Squinting, I shook my head to rid the shroud of pain that engulfed me, causing a shot of fiery agony to rip through my body, but it cleared my muddled thoughts.

Gritting my teeth, I peered from my hideout. The grass glistened in the morning sun. I licked my dry lips. Cool water. I longed for a drink to ease the heat raging inside me. I yowled as I rose. Cramps grabbed my front leg and twisted me, wrenching my stomach into a knot. My tummy convulsed in a futile attempt to rid itself of its misery. I collapsed.

ACTIVATE LION MODE

Darkness rescued me, carrying me back to my happy place. Visons floated in my head of me curled up in the bedcovers next to Judy. I dreamed I led Judy down a path in the forest, showing her the tall grasses and big leaves ... and a grasshopper! The fantasies scrolled by. Judy fed me my favorite treats. I lay on her lap, massaging her tummy with my paws and purring. She kissed me on the nose. We played hide and seek. I played the 'Boo! Game'.

Katie ghostly form appeared. She hung in the mist at the end of a long tunnel with her friend Destiny, who lived with the angels. The girls' laughter chimed like silver bells. Katie floated nearer, shaking her finger as her mother had probably done to her many times. Her small voice was low and serious. "You can't come with us, Sportster. You have to go back." How did she know my name? She used to call me Mittens. I obeyed, walking back the way I had come. My shoulder didn't hurt.

Jawbreaker's hot breath brushed my face. I opened my eyes. He was no dream. Nudging me, he pushed his nose under my chin. His slobbery tongue swept across my face, soaking it. His dog breath made my eyes pop open. He wanted me to get up. I tried but didn't get up. He slathered me with one more big, wet kiss, barked, and ran away. I closed my eyes and slipped back, hoping to find Katie and Destiny.

Again, the voices woke me. "Easy now." Hands lifted me up. I cried out, but no sound came from my dry throat. The pain pulsed constantly now. I gave in to the darkness. Judy's scent surrounded me like a warm blanket.

ACTIVATE LION MODE

CHAPTER THIRTY-EIGHT

I hovered near the ceiling in the corner. Was that me? Mom held my paw as I lay on the cold steel table. She was crying. The doctor that I had hissed and spat at stood by her side. "I've patched him up and set his leg. It's up to the little guy, now."

I hate it when they call me that.

"His paw moved! I felt it!" Mom's face, full of hope, looked up at the Doc.

"It's just a reflex. He won't be waking up yet." He took Mom's hand and steered her to the door. "It's up to him and his Cat Gods. They know how many lives he has left."

They exited the room, leaving my lifeless form to the quiet breathing machines. I didn't hurt anymore. I was in a sweet, quiet place that smelled of Judy. I felt strangely better, yet I was very tired. So very tired. I wanted to quit. I had lived a good life. Judy had taken me places and shown me things, no other cat could have imagined. The White Sands of New Mexico. The largest litter box ever! And the oceans, both The Pacific and the Atlantic. Every California cat I'd ever met had never chased the tides or waded the tide pools. And the dogs

~~JUDY HOWARD~~ SPORTSTER THE CAT

I've taunted at the grooming shop, yes, I have lived a good life.

Katie and Destiny, again, stood at the end of the mist-filled tunnel talking with an older girl. I called to them. I wanted to ask if they had seen Judy. The older girl separated from the group and glided through the tunnel's fog toward me.

She was in her twenties. Her hair was like a black cotton hat and matched her dark eyes. Her skin glowed as if she were a bronze goddess. "My name is Crystal. I was a friend of Wendy's."

I must have looked confused.

She smiled and picked me up. "We were homies. I was in Blade's stable."

Blade? Wendy? Blade was dead. And Wendy...? I twitched my tail and chirped, as I glanced down to see my lifeless form still on the stainless steel table.

"I wanted to thank you for saving Wendy," she said. Her voice reminded me of a music box. "You did such a courageous deed. Girls like me and Wendy, we don't have many friends we can trust. You know? Tell her I'm in a better place now, will you? If you go back." She kissed me on the nose. "I hope you go back. You have so much more living to do."

She set me down and began walking back to join Katie and Destiny. "Wait!" I yelled, but she didn't hear. The tunnel vanished in a swoosh and I found myself still hovering over the table, peering down on the cat that looked like me. I closed my eyes that I hadn't opened and slept.

***

I tried to fight my way back to the room but instead I drifted in foggy unconsciousness. Visions of warm, fleece sweatshirts competed against, thundering nightmares that sent screeches like the sound of twisted metal up my spine. Towering shadows growled, panting their hot, rank breaths at me and flashing fangs like lightning. My body shivered and my brain demanded my legs to flee. Yet, I slept. I shifted between the pull of Judy's memory and the push of yearning to join Katie and her friend, Destiny in their cool, soothing mist.

***

Voices filtered with soft music. "We just have to wait and see. …The antibiotics have to do their job. His fever is very high… If we can't get it down …."

"How soon will you know?" It was Mom's voice.

"I'm sorry, it's too soon to tell. It's only been twenty-four hours. I just don't know." The doctor hung his head. "It could go either way at this point."

"He wasn't eating before this happened. Did you find anything else wrong? I wanted to bring him in two days ago, but Ralph….."

The doctor held his palm up. "No there's nothing else. He's probably depressed and he's underweight, which isn't helping. I heard you found his owner. What's going on with that?"

"The woman is recovering from an accident in her motorhome in the Olympic Forest. She's at the Forks Community Hospital in Washington. She was in intensive care for days. By the time, she came to, and asked about her cat, he was long gone. People posted flyers, but nothing. She thought he was dead. His name's Sportster."

"The Olympic Forest? He's come a long way. I'll bet he has a story to tell." The doc scratched some notes on his clipboard. The doctor's solemn voice lightened. "But she's coming for him, right?"

"She's been moved to a rehab facility. They say any day now she'll be able to travel."

The doc's voice turned serious again. "If she were here …," he made some more notes. "The problem is those three days in the park after he was hit with no medical treatment ….." He shook his head. "I just don't know."

"But …"

"I'm sorry. I wish I could give you more hope, Mrs. Meeker, but you have to prepare your daughter for the worst. Sportster may not make it."

****

ACTIVATE LION MODE

I barely felt the prick of the needle as the girl chattered. I wish everyone would leave me alone "You better come around soon, Sportster. It's been two days already. Your fans have turned our parking lot into a tailgating vigil. The amount of flowers and cat toys folks have sent or dropped off has filled a corner of the reception area. You can' let them down. And the money! They're talking of starting a foundation in your honor. The Feline Fury Foundation. How do you like the sound of that?" She held up the vial, marked on it, and then started to leave. Pausing, she bent down and kissed my lifeless form. As she fluffed up the fleeced sweatshirt, I lay on, suddenly my heart sputtered, and then beat rapidly. It was Judy's sweatshirt! She's here! She came for me!

****

How much time had passed? I didn't know. I activated lion mode. In my mind, I scratched and clawed to fight the heaviness weighting me down. I growled and spat, arguing with my own defeating thoughts of giving up. Judy was nearby. I was sure of it. When exhaustion from the internal battle, I fought over came me, I slept, snuggled deep in Judy's sweatshirt. It was almost like being home on her bed, waiting to play peek-a-boo. Almost.

The next morning the doctor stood over me, again with Mom and Ralph flanking him. "I expect he'll gain consciousness any day now. He began improving as soon as you wrapped him with the woman's sweatshirt. Who thought of that?"

"I have a friend from nursing school who works in Rehab at Forks Community. She's the one who found Sportster's owner, right under her nose. She overnighted the sweat shirt to me, figuring it might help."

"We still have to get him to eat. If he eats, he can go home. Animals are like people. Sometimes the road to recovery is too steep, and they just give up. Even if he overcomes the infection, he still has to deal with the cast on his leg and the pain from his cracked ribs."

"This cat's special. He's a fighter, like a lion. He's made it this far." That was Ralph's voice.

"He certainly has his fans. The flowers and cards just keep coming."

"We've been taking the flowers over to the women's shelter," Ralph said.

"The cash donations have more than paid my bill. How's the Feline Foundation coming along?"

"There's over $5,000.00 dollars so far. We're thinking of creating a scholarship for battered women."

Mom's fingers caressed me on my head. I meowed but no sound reached my ears.

ACTIVATE LION MODE

CHAPTER THIRTY-NINE

A dog whined. My eyes fluttered open. Soft warm blankets cradled me but the harsh smell of medicine alarmed me. Adrenaline rushed through my veins and I struggled to stand Instead, I belted out an intended roar that resulted in a whimper. A sterile smelling girl sitting in the corner jumped from her chair and approached.

"It's all right, Sportster. You're going to be fine." She opened the barred door of my enclosure and ran her fingers lightly over my head.

Encouraged by her kindness, I summoned every bit of energy to rise, but my front leg would not cooperate. Sniffing at the offending, aching limb, I licked at it. My leg was hard and numb. Mewing, I looked up, pleading for the girl to remove the restriction.

"I know, little guy, but you're going to have to wear that bothersome cast for a while, 'til your leg heals."

I butted my head against her hand then stumbled over to the dishes in the corner of my cage. Passing over the kibble, I lapped up some water. The coolness slid down my throat and pooled in my tummy. I drank and drank. Exhausted and hurting from the effort, I collapsed in front of the dishes. The girl lifted me up and laid me back upon the blankets.

"You rest. You've had a rough time. You were a very sick cat when they found you. I'm sure you have used up one of your nine lives." She shoved some sweet tasting stuff in my mouth. "This is for your pain," she said, continuing to pet me. I licked at it, closed my eyes and sensing I was safe, faded off to my happy place.

When my eyes fluttered opened again, the room swirled. Inhaling the chemical odors, I remembered where I was. The scent of water in the drinking bowl caused me to lick my dry lips. Teetering, I stood up. Taking one-step forward, I fell forward on my chin. My right leg remained as if glued to the cage floor. Pain spiked through my jaw and my ribs ached, making it hard to breathe. I collapsed where I stood. My toes peeked out of a hard, heavy thing wrapped around my right leg. I yowled and attempted to shake it off. Trobbing cramps shot through my chest, and unable to catch my breath, my yowl turned into a kitten's mew.

The doctor, smelling like medicine, entered the room. I wanted to bite him, but sensed he only wanted to help. Anyway, I was in no condition to argue. He was probably here to get this weight off my leg. I let out another little mew.

ACTIVATE LION MODE

"Look at you, Sportster. You must be feeling better."

I meowed louder, though I didn't want to seem demanding.

He ignored me as he unhooked the clipboard hanging on my cage. "Looks like your fever's gone down." He opened the crate's door. Yes! He lifted me up, carried me to the cold steel examining table, probably to better figure out how to get the tree stump off my leg.

When he stuck something cold up my butt. I abandoned my truce and spat at him. I tried to leap from the table, but my stump leg kept me grounded. He quickly removed the cold thing then lifted my lips and examined my mouth. "Your color is back, Sportster. You're going to be going home soon. I'll have the chef at this here hotel bring you something tasty from the kitchen. If you eat today you might go home tomorrow."

He gave me a quick pat on the head and placed me back in my cage. Wait! The stump! Aren't you going to get rid of it? He slid the latch closed, and I bellowed out a loud, demanding meow. How could this be happening? I can't stay here! Suddenly aware of the scent of sickness, I tuned into the dogs' cries and whimpers. I could not ignore the lingering odor of death either. I steeled against the shooting cramps and yowled even louder. Pain cut my plea short. I twitched my tail, arched my back and let out a lion's roar.

~~JUDY HOWARD~~ SPORTSTER THE CAT

As yummy as the food smelled I only sniffed it. I can't eat when I'm angry. Instead, I curled up in the corner the best I could with the stump on my leg and went to sleep.

CHAPTER FORTY

I slept most of the morning until the doctor woke me. "Good morning, Sportster, I brought visitors to see you."

The sound of my own name cheered me. I was tired of everyone calling me, Little Guy, or Mittens, or Cat. I hobbled to the front of the cage.

I mewed at the familiar faces of Mom and Ralph. "Hey, Little Guy. Oops sorry. I meant Sportster." Mom said as she poked her finger through the bars. "Where did you get such a name?" I sniffed her finger and rubbed my head against it. Didn't she know a Sportster was a Harley Davidson motorcycle? It's a badass name, like Leo The Lion.

"Look here, we brought yummies." She removed the lid from a dish of tuna she had brought from home.

I sniffed the morsels as the doctor opened the door and lifted me onto the exam table again. Oh no! Not the butt thing again.

Mom set the small dish on the table. "If you eat this, the doc says you can check out of this place."

I sniffed it. My tummy growled.

Ralph said, "Come on, Sportster. Eat for Carolyn. She wants you to be home when she gets out of school today.

I sniffed again, and then took a nibble. Forgetting my anger, I gobbled it all down and licked the dish clean. I gazed up and meowed at Mom.

"That's all there is, but there's more at home." Mom glanced up at the doc, who nodded so she said, "You see? That was your ticket out of here. Let's go home."

Doc petted me on the head and said, "The staff's going to miss you, Sportster, but I need to ask for one favor before we release you."

Mom scooped me up. "Anything," she said. "We're so grateful for all you've done. You saved Sportster's life."

"There're several reporters in the reception area and a man from the National Park Service."

Mom met Doc's gaze. "The National Park Service? What does he want?"

"I think they all just want pictures and a report on Sportster's progress. Do you mind?" Doc said.

"Of course not." Mom scratched my ears. "We owe at least that much to his fans."

What? Pictures with this stump leg? I squirmed to escape.

"Wait 'til we get home, Sportster," Ralph said. "Then you can get used to walking with your cast. Come on. Let's go meet your public."

We entered the crowded reception area packed with reporters and clients with their pets. The cameras flashed and the applause startled me. I buried my eyes in Mom's arms.

"Mrs. Meeker, how is Cat?" I pulled my head up. It was Janet, the Alabama Coon Hound reporter and her associate Garcia.

"Cat has a name. It's Sportster," Mom said. I butted my head against her. Thank you. "He suffered a broken leg and cracked ribs when the car hit him," Mom began. "And then he crawled off and hid in the park bushes for three days before we found him. He was a very sick cat, but he was lucky. As you can see he's recovering nicely."

"We heard a Pit Bull found him," Janet said as she made notes.

Mom nodded. "Yes, after the motorhome accident, Sportster befriended two homeless veterans living in the Olympic forest with their dog named Pit, but the cat had moved on probably trying to find his real owner. When they had heard about Cat in the news and came to our house to give him a home."

Janet reached out and ran her fingers lightly over me while Garcia snapped a photo and jotted down more notes.

"You're right, Janet," Mom said. "If it hadn't been for their dog, Pit, we probably wouldn't have found him. Sportster was near dead when Pit found him."

"When do we meet his owner, Judy?"

I jerked my head around. Judy?

The man's voice was deep and spoke with a slow drawl. His blue eyes were shrouded by his broad rimmed hat. He handed Ralph a card. "My name is Mr. Gearing. I'm a representative of the National Park Service. We heard about this cat's adventures all the way in Dc." Digging into his pocket, he pulled out a few treats between his fingers. "Is it okay to give him a treat?"

I reached for the man's offer, the man who had mentioned my Judy's name.

"As a representative of national park service I would like to meet with Sportster and Judy when it's convenient."

The mention of her name sent an ache through me not caused by my stump leg or broken ribs. I bellowed a meow.

~~JUDY HOWARD~~ SPORTSTER THE CAT

The crowd burst into laughter. I hissed. What's so funny?

CHAPTER FORTY-ONE

Mom carried me to the car while Ralph talked to the reporters for a few moments.

At home as promised, Mom dished up more tuna. Ralph placed me gently on the floor.

Still ravenous, I shoved pride aside, hopped clumsily to my bowl, and scarfed down the food. Unable to raise my stump leg to wipe my face when finished, I cleaned only half my mug. I sat, licking my lips just as the side door banged shut and Carolyn burst into the kitchen.

She threw her books on the table and spotting me said, "Hello Cat!" Dropping to her knees, she scooped me up. "I'm sorry. My bad. I forgot. Your name's Sportster."

Purring I rubbed against her chin and she kissed me on the nose."

They had returned to the house with me wrapped in Judy's sweatshirt. She had to be close. The scent of her sent a newfound energy charging through me at the possibility of seeing her. I had to continue my search. I was more determined than ever. So much time had been wasted. Stump leg or not, my blood pulsed and my tail twitched anxiously from a feeling of urgency. I imagined myself snuggled in her lap while we watched TV. No one knew how to kiss me on the top of my head like she did. I envisioned her surprise when I would wake her from the forgetfulness of sleep on our first morning together. Her eyes would widen as wakefulness reminded her I was home.

I dragged my stump leg through the house, making sure the cage of death was gone. In the living room, I made a clumsy attempt to jump up onto the windowsill but failed, and I fell back on my rump. I sat a few moments, staring up, hoping someone would come along and lift me up. No one came. After two more tries, I succeeded. I do my best thinking when I can look outside and see freedom.

A sweet aroma of a cake baking curled out of the oven and into the living room. Carolyn and Mom hustled in the kitchen. The doorbell rang over the rattling pans in the kitchen.

Ralph opened the door to Tatooman, Guitarman and Mr .Gearing. "Hello gentlemen. You're early. The reunion party doesn't start for a couple of hours yet."

Guitarman spoke up. " We know we just thought we could help set up for the party." He glanced over at Mr. Gearing.

"Yes sir. Me, too. I was just trying to kill time in my motel room. I guess we all had the same idea. I can help out for an hour and then have to return to the motel for a conference call. I'll be able to come back for the party. I'll just be about forty-five minutes late."

Ralph swung the door open wide. "Come on in gentlemen. This old man I can use the help."

Ralph spoke over the clatter. "I'll get the extension cord from the storage shed, so she can park alongside the house and plug in her motorhome," He motioned to the men. "Come on out to the garage and I'll show you where the tables are. You can set them up in the back yard. We sure appreciate your help."

The two veterans nodded. "We're happy to help out. We just want the cat to get back with his rightful owner. He deserves it. He's a special cat. He's touched so many lives."

Ralph paused before he headed out to the garage. "I understand you're both studying criminal justice." He reached in his pocket and pulled out a card. "Here. After everything settles down with the cat, come see me at the station. I'll get you hooked up with jobs that will fit with your school schedules."

The veterans nodded and each grabbed Ralph's hand, shaking it vigorously. "Thank you, Mr. Meeker. Thank you, so much."

As the men made their way to the garage, the clatter in the kitchen quieted. "The spaghetti sauce will be perfect by the time she gets here, at six right?" Carolyn said. "We need to run to the store for garlic bread."

"We'll go while the cake cools," Mom said.

"Sportster' going to be so surprised," Carolyn's voice reminded me of Katie.

I plotted my strategy as I peered out the window. If they are planning a party for me, they were going to be disappointed. I expected to be on the road by dusk, and only travel in the safety of darkness. No more pussy footing around. No more falling for the good intentions of some kind-hearted person to feed me and offer me a warm place to sleep. And I certainly would not be tricked by some do-gooder taking pity on me and then dumping me at the shelter again. Judy was close. There was no time to waste.

I jumped from the window and gulped air from the pain that shot up my leg. Just as quickly, my sore ribs squeezed the air from my lungs.t I ducked behind the curtain and curled up for a nap before I began the last leg of my adventure.

The familiar tinkle of keys woke me. Mom and Carolyn were getting ready to go to the store. I snuck into the laundry room and hunched down between the washer and the wall near the door. I hoped to be able to maneuver my stump leg and dash out and down the side of the house without being noticed.

Mom, pulled open the back door, paused, and turning back to Carolyn said, "I almost forgot, grab the recycle bags, sweetheart."

It was a cinch. I made it out and around the corner before they closed the door. Judy is close. I felt her in my aching bones. All I had to do was be careful.

I waited in the bushes until Mom's taillights disappeared down the street. The going was not easy as I crept along, trying to keep a low profile. Each step I took my stump leg hit the sidewalk with a thunk, but I managed a steady pace, clump, clump, and clump.

I by-passed the park. That would be the first place they would look for me. Moving off the sidewalk, I sneaked from yard to yard, from rose bush, to flower bed, and under cars parked in the driveways. The going was slow, but I remained vigilant, always waiting and watching. The night wore on.

I reached the strip mall and carefully crossed the street. It was difficult to keep a slow pace, because my excitement pushed me on. Sprinting from one parked car to the next, reflected images of passing vehicles wiggled across the storefront windows. One took on the shape of Judy's motorhome. My heart flip-flopped, but I reminded myself it was only an illusion, like the cat in the mirror at home.

ACTIVATE LION MODE

Dawn was breaking by the time I reached the corner, which was one block from the freeway entrance. I crept behind a Mexican restaurant and snuck under the gate of an enclosure for a trash bin. It would be safe to rest here for a few hours.

I wondered how the party turned out. I'll bet Judy will throw a party for me when I find her. She always threw a party on my birthday. We shared the same birthday. Our friends from the grooming shop brought me toys and catnip, and Judy fed me a special Fancy feast dinner, like what Annabelle's folks fed her every day.

She will probably cry. She cries when she's happy. I hope she hasn't thrown away my bed that looks like a tiger, or my favorite catnip mouse she gave me, "for no reason except because I am the best," she said.

As the black sky faded, turning to a cloudy grey, he glow of the street lights dimmed and popped off

Unable to overcome my unexplained anticipation and sleep, I ignored my rule to travel only at night. I would cover the one block distance to the freeway ramp, and then follow the ditch running beside the southbound lane. I crawled out from under the trash bin and, arching my back, I stretched. A quiet rain dotted the asphalt.

My legs, stiff from dragging the encumbrance attached to my leg, caused me to stumble as I made my way around to the front of the strip mall. Sitting down, I chewed on the pasty cast, trying to pull it off, and then growled at my lack of progress. I shook off the moisture beginning to soak my fur. Hissing, I spit at nothing in particular, and then shot toward the sidewalk that led to the corner by the freeway ramp.

No longer quiet, the rain pounded the vehicles as they splashed through the pooling puddles, flooding the gutters. Head down, eyes squinted almost shut, I kept a pace of determination down the sidewalk. A car behind a motorhome blared its horn over the downpour, startling me. I glanced up. Was it the illusion from last night's storefront window? The deluge washed away any scent of the motorhome, which maneuvered to the curb and parked. Again, the car behind it sounded its horn, forcing me to dash away from its ear-piercing peal. I escaped back into the parking lot and dove into a line of bushes, but not before a curtain of dirty, cold water flooded over me as a car sped past.

Shivering and frightened, I hunkered down into the mud. How was I ever going to get home? Maybe the infection was back. I thought I was hallucinating, seeing motorhomes that I wished were Judy's. I whimpered a kitten meow. I decided to return to the trash bin enclosure and wait out the storm. I tried to take a step. The soaked stump leg was now twice as heavy as it had been. I howled in frustration.

I howled again, and again. I couldn't go on. Over the thundering cadence of the raindrops, a faint voice called my name, not once, but twice. I held my breath.

And again! It wasn't just a voice. It was Judy's! It sounded so real. I poked my head past the bushes and shook my head to clear the water from my eyes. A woman splashed through water, which now rushed by like a torrential river. Could I dare to hope?

"Sportster!"

It was Judy! I bolted toward the shadowy form. The leaden stump too heavy to lift, I used the strength in my other legs and dragged the leg like a ball and chain through the mud and the muck.

"Sportster!" Her voice was clear and loud. There was no doubt. I panted from the exertion. I thought my chest would burst. I paused to catch my breath when I heard Judy scream.

~~JUDY HOWARD~~ SPORTSTER THE CAT

CHAPTER FORTY-TWO

The car barreled toward her, like a fish hawk sweeping down on its prey.

Activate lion mode!

As I had done for Carolyn when she was in the clutches of Blade, I reacted. Pumped with feline fury, I leaped through the air. I slammed into Judy, square on her chest. The heaviness of my stump leg doubled my weight and I hit hard. She toppled, plunging back onto the slippery asphalt that now raged like rapids. Clinging to her chest, I rode with her as she hit the ground. The speeding car propelled on by, missing us by a cat's hair, but sending another deluge of oily, black water cascading over the both of us.

Nothing else mattered. I had found Judy. Her arms wrapped around me and I inhaled her lavender scent. "Sportster, I found you." She was sobbing.

I told you, she would cry. We sat in the dark pools of water as another car swooshed past, drenching us yet again.

She laughed out loud, over the pounding rain, the honking horns and my happy chirping. Struggling to her feet and stumbling, she carried me, to the motorhome. She held me tightly as she climbed inside. I rubbed against her face, purring and chirping.

Lost in the joy of our reunion, we both jumped when the dark figure of a man tapped on the driver's window, interrupting our wondrous reunion. Water dripped from the man's broad rimmed hat. His dark complexion accented his silver hair that was plastered against his temples. When he wiped the rain from his eyes, the street lamp caught the blue color of his eyes.

"Ma'am, are you all right?"

Laughing and crying Judy rolled down the window. She wiped tears from her own eyes and cried even harder. "Yes," she said. "I'm fine."

He frowned. "Ma'am, are you sure?" He tried to peer into the motorhome. "Are you alone?"

Choking back sobs, she said, "Not anymore. This is the best day of my life." She kissed me on my head. Her hair dripped down in scraggled waves. Black smudges discolored her cheeks like a bad rouge. I beamed up at her as she caught her breath.

"Meet Sportster," she said. "He just risked his life to save mine. Last week even at gunpoint, he saved a little girl's life, I don't know how many lives he has left, but I guarantee I'm going to be spending the rest of mine making sure he stays safe. I'm not letting this little guy out of my sight."

~~JUDY HOWARD~~ SPORTSTER THE CAT

Little guy? Really? After all I've done?

The man's eyes lit up with recognition. "This is Sportster! I just came from the Meeker's house. I wanted to meet you and Sportster. I must have just missed you. I've been following his story. I even donated to his veterinary bill. Congratulations ma'am." He reached out his hand. "I am so happy you have him back."

Judy reached past me and shook the man's hand. "It is nice to meet you. And thank you for the donation. I will pay you back."

"Oh no ma'am, that's okay. I'm so happy to meet you. I'm with the National Park Service." He pulled a card from his pocket and handed it to Judy. We heard about Sportster back in DC and found his adventures quite the human-interest story. The National Park Service is looking for a spokesperson, a mascot, if you will. You remember Smokey The Bear, don't you?" He paid no mind to the rain drizzling down from his wide brimmed hat.

Judy took his card, read the text and said, "What does that have to do with Sportster?"

"We would like Sportster to be the mascot for the National Park Service."

I butted my head against her chin. Say yes! What an opportunity! I could roam every national park in the country. What an adventure! Activate lion mode! Why is she hesitating?

"I don't know what to say." She examined the card again, "Mr. Gearing."

"Like I said. I just came from the Meeker's Reunion party they had planned for you and Sportster. They said explained how Sportster had run off again and that you had just left."

Judy laughed. "It's hard to have a reunion without the main participant. My heart was broken that he had run away again. I was ready to give up and head back to California."

Mr. Gearing scanned the shopping center. "Is there somewhere we can talk?"

"I don't know." She gazed down at me, scratching and petting me, "I can't leave him. I mean I can, but just not right now." And I need to go back to the Meeker's. They're going to be so surprised."

"You go ahead, turn around. Tell them the happy reunion happened in the pouring rain of a strip mall." The man's smile lit up his dark complexion and the lamplight turned his dark blue eyes to hazel. "I'll text them, give them a heads up we're on our way."

Yes! Activate Lion Mascot Mode!

ABOUT THE AUTHOR

The death of Judy Howard's husband gave the soon to be author a wakeup call, reminding her that life is short. After discovering her gift of writing, Howard sold her pet grooming business, which she had operated since the age of elven and engaged full throttle into her new passions of writing and traveling.

Judy Howard's writing career expands across many genres, including memoir, romantic mystery, reality fiction, travel and young adult, but the theme is always the same - overcoming life's difficulties.

Sportster, the cat accompanies Judy in their Winnebago motorhome as she travels across the country writing, lecturing and presenting seminars.

Missing the excitement of working at the pet salon, Sportster pounced into his own new career as a talented ghostwriter with his first book, ACTIVATE LION MODE. He is busy scratching out the second book in his Feline Fury Series.

When Judy and Sportster are not traveling, they reside at their desert home in Sun City, California

ACTIVATE LION MODE

CONTACT JUDY HOWARD

WEBSITE:
WWW.JUDYHOWARDPUBLISHING.COM

EMAIL: JHOWARD1935@GMAIL.COM

Made in the USA
Columbia, SC
06 September 2017